LEAST
of
THESE
LEAST

BY

LANCELOT
SCHAUBERT

Copyright © 2022 by Lancelot Schaubert
All rights reserved.

Schaubert, Lancelot
Least of These Least / Lancelot Schaubert
ISBN-13: 978-1-949547-08-5
1. RELIGION / Christian Theology / Ethics
2. RELIGION / Christian Living / Social Issues
3. RELIGION / Spirituality
I. New York City
II. Joplin, Missouri
Printed in the United States of America

Because the thing you hear in books like *When Helping Hurts* or in stories about pulling yourself up by your bootstraps and "God helps those who help themselves," is that some of the hungry did it to themselves. Some are dehydrating themselves and poisoning the water holes of their community. Some are naked cause they're nudists or in the BDSM voyeur crowd or because they're selling their clothes for drugs. Some are undocumented migrants because they're escaping crimes they committed, because they're running from their calling like Jonah, because they're running drugs, or homeless because they love the adventure of sleeping rough. Some are in prison because they're guilty.

They're the least.

They *deserved* it.

Jesus says that's him.

What have you done for *him **through** the ones you have every right to hate, shame, mistrust, and avoid? Through the ones you have **good cause** to be bitter towards?*

That should bother you.

The Malnourished.

St. Paul said if a man does not work he will not eat. Yet Jesus fed the five thousand for free. How do we square those?

Well for starters, the implication of having fed the five thousand indiscriminately (they returned again and again to Jesus for more food, so indiscriminately that it was something like ten to twenty thousand with women and children) shows that he gave bread and loaves to those hungry *least deserving* of a free meal. And then turns and tells us to do the same is to give food to him.

It seems a solidarity... no, a sympathy... no, an empathy... no: a *compassion* exists between those who suffer in any form and Jesus. Suffering is so qualitatively evil — being and existence so qualitatively good — to feed the hungry, any hungry, is to expand upon God's primitive creative act, to participate in incarnation, to root on the sustaining presence of the Holy Spirit. At that Holy Spirit's entrance into the Creed my bride tends to shout like a little girl, "THE LORD! THE GIVER OF LIFE! WHO PROCEEDS FROM THE FATHER AND THE SON! WHO WITH THE SON IS ADORED AND GLORIFIED! WHO HAS SPOKEN THROUGH THE PROPHETS!" To feed the hungry, any hungry, roots out the qualitative evil of hunger: of non-being manifested in starvation. Even fasting holds no permanence in and on the human soul, for we use it merely to tame our restless gluttony, the hunger at the opposite end of the culinary spectrum as any bulimic worth his salt knows. Gluttony is an others-consuming hunger. Anorexia, the self.

So who are the least among the hungry?

Those who have every reason to be full.

And yet Jesus says if you feed the least hungerer, you feed Jesus.

Why?

When The Son identified himself with man, he took on "whatever death the Father wished to send him with all its anguish, pain, and sorrow." From hunger in the desert to the "I thirst" on the cross, to Rich Mullins's line — *he did not have a home: there were places he visited frequently, took off his shoes and scratched his feet cause he knew that the whole world belonged to the meek so he did not have a home* — Jesus knows the five worst pains. Exposure. Starvation. Dehydration. Illness. Imprisonment. They say, ultimately, that everyone dies from asphyxia: lack of air to the brain. There's really five ways to be strangled: a lack of sugar and protein to convey oxygen to the brain, a lack of fluids to do so, an exposure so that raiders or beasts or the sun take more from your brain than you can put back in, a foreign body taking over yours (think: zombie virus), or — the worst — other humans take the breath of God from your dust.

The sin of Cain.

And that's the key: over and over again, these five acts, five abyssal states, stand in wholehearted opposition to the Creator and Sustainer and Author of Life. If you, through passivity or activity, increase hunger, thirst, exposure, sickness, and exile, *at all*, Jesus says you're on team death.

Wrong team, pro lifer.

Doesn't matter if the person in front of you is on team death and deserves, both because of how they treat themselves and others, to die a brutal death. It seems that God made it clear through Jesus's life that in the final estimation, we are not the sort of creatures who merely bodily die, but rather who bodily rise and live forever in newness of life. Once you realize that, you stop sinning in order to delay death. Death entered the world, whereupon all sinned says Paul in Romans.

And that's exactly how we treat people: they *might* expedite our own death — the specific death we fear with our own specific phobia — and we therefore sin against other sinners. Death increases and, with it, so increases the number of people desperate to ward off their inevitable demise and the demise of their everything. They end up adding yet more death. Death's the root of every phobia. Fear of crowds is fear of death by stoning, heights of falling, spiders of biting, speeds of crashing, germs of… well… COVID. Or the Black Plague. And other diseases. With that fear and anger and shame comes sin to ward it off at all costs: *if it's between you and me, bub, I choose me.*

I look out for numero uno.

But Jesus does the opposite. He not only embraces his death and demise — his most consistent sermon was "I'm going to die. Young. And soon." He put himself in positions where he *knew* others would take advantage of him. Did it anyways. That's sort of the gist behind, "If someone asks you for a loan, give it. And don't expect repayment." *Ever*, he implies.

The word for that is a gift. A grant without the proper requisition form or grant writer. Grace.

Jesus knew he could set down his life and pick it up again as the first fruits of the resurrection. Jesus's death and dying becomes not something to merely accept after the stages of grief. It moves beyond Kübler Ross to become one more tool in Jesus's arsenal for gracing the world with his presence. He doesn't mind dying, illness, sleeping rough, fasting, thirsting, or being imprisoned *for someone else* to have life, bed, food, water, freedom.

Anyone else. Yes, *that* anyone, the one person you wish didn't count in the category "brotherhood of man."

Are there systemic problems and addictions that might need more long term solutions?

Fascinating question. I'll do you one better:

Does the previous question cut out the heart of the giver? Does the question *"when does helping hurt?"* make it any less good to give to the most hungry or the person who deserves food the least? Can *that very question* corrupt the heart of the doer, the giver, the donator, the sacrificer so that they can't let go of, say, thirty pieces of silver or some expensive perfume?

In short: did practical questions corrupt Judas?

One of the largest men I have ever had the pleasure of knowing was a 400 pound opera critic named Paul. Paul was Shakespeare's Falstaff: big, boisterous, loud, an infinite repository and generator of interesting anecdotes. (Simpsons. Dio. Red Socks. Wagner). Wherever Paul went, he made friends and enemies. Every storefront in our Brooklyn neighborhood had an opinion about Paul: they either loved or hated the guy. Some regretted hating him, long term.

I loved him. Adored and respected him and to this day retain unconditional confidence in him.

However, he was a very messy eater. And a big one. And he ate a ton. And he never lacked for food. One fine June day in summer of 2019, I walked through my Brooklyn neighborhood to a central European cafe named Slímak — the place where Paul and a British-educated Nicaraguan sailor named Junior had taught me Shogi. A couple years later Junior would call me and tell me to call the coast guard because he had sunk his ship off the coast of City Island. Junior hadn't shown that day either. Paul sat alone that day, big opera critic alone in a central European cafe booth sipping his farm-to-cup coffee. He didn't need my help with a meal, either buying it or eating it, but I bought him one. And I got one myself and sat down to eat across from him and talk. Our conversation wandered and he ended up asking me if I had seen Wagner's *Ring Cycle*.

"I've seen exactly one opera, Paul. *La Bohème*. That's qualitatively more than most dudes."

"Do you know the story?" he asked.

I shook my head.

"Do you want to?"

I had appointments that day. Books that needed writing. All sorts of busy things. The ghost of Nouwen looked on: *the interruptions are your work*, he whispered. "Yes," I said in spite of myself. "Yes, I want to."

3 HOURS LATER:

I now had the totality of the plot of *a trilogy of operas* in my head. One that, turns out, both George Lucas and John Williams stole from for Star Wars, not to mention any genre with "opera" in the name. Or heavy metal. I could still recite it, more or less. I walked Paul to the 36th street subway and he asked as he was leaving where I was traveling.

"Joplin," I said. "Teaching at a creative arts academy."

"Anything else?"

"Visiting family and supporters," I said. "Probably six states."

"For how long?"

"Five weeks."

"Woah," he said, "that's a long time."

"Yeah," I said, "But I'll come back and we'll watch some Wagner."

Thursday of Creative Arts Academy in Joplin, Paul had a massive heart attack and was dead in thirty minutes. I'm glad whatever you think he deserved, large as he was, I had bought him one last meal and learned about opera from him one last time. He was hungry. Food made it less hard when he passed.

I met Jesus, in retrospect, through Paul.

Ronald Rolheiser tells us in his *Holy Longing* that Princess Diana stands halfway between Janis Joplin and Mother Theresa, between a deep disintegrating indulgence and a deeply integrated sacrifice. She suffered from severe bulimia and anorexia: in my experience, the hardest person to feed is someone who starves themselves. And not in the strategic ascetic or religious sense: starving themselves for looks or their relationship with food. Often while watching *The Crown* I wondered: had Diana been properly invited *by her husband or mother-in-law* into the table fellowship of the royal family whom she so deeply cherished, would things have turned out differently for her?

Had her own husband enjoyed a meal with her more often, would she have eaten herself from the inside out?

We had a neighbor who struggled with suicide and anorexia and addiction who had no right to a meal by the standards of the world. But we had her over for dinner and celebrated her sobriety and though that wasn't everything — though that was hardly *anything* — that spirit of sustenance helped her who starved herself.

Starving from natural causes is supposed to be painless.

Is starving yourself because your family won't eat with you?

Starving, by the grace of God, is supposed to be one of the gentlest ways to die assuming you aren't binge-purging yourself to death. Something happens in the mind of a starving child and a sort of euphoria takes over. Your body stops taking food. Mold grows on your trachea and you stop feeling pain.

But in a world full of so many foodies and plenty of food for all, why must anyone starve?

Hoarding.

Binging and purging.

Especially because of those who do not deserve to have a meal from their neglect to properly distribute what exists.

There lives a man experiencing homelessness on my street. Will. At the time I'm talking about, Will took more free handouts without actually going through the system than anyone I have encountered in New York. And we have beggars galore, enough that Tara and I once asked a church to donate 200 pharmacy gift cards in the amount of $5 so we would have something to offer folks. You get tired of saying "no" in NYC, but especially for cash. That helps. But Will subsists off of the discarded lotto tickets and the leftovers and the tuna surprise that the guys at the Jackie Gleason Depot offer him. He's mentally disabled and old and multiple times got a chance off the street. Does he deserve a meal?

I mean he gets them free all the time and doesn't work.

Yet we invite him over for our brunches when we have them and guess what?

When he shows, it radically humanizes the folks there. The fashion stylist of Elle once sat across the same table and it actually helped them both. Because she is hungry and thirsty for righteousness and him for real food. She is poor of spirit and he's straight-up poor. They need each other, you see, and wouldn't realize it without table fellowship. They're both just as lonely, thinking about what the other person deserves.

🦴 · 🍷 · 🏠 · 👤 · 🚗 · 🎙️

A rich kid. Their family bought me meals all the time growing up. I love this family: they're the reason I could get extra allowance by pocketing what my mom had given me for paying for my meal. My family had a ton of pride on the pay-for-your-meals front. Dignity. Shame when they discovered I hadn't paid and the rich family had.

I came back to my hometown later in life and knew, still, they did not need — they least deserved — for someone to buy them dinner.

And yet...

After a bathroom break, I did it anyways. I snuck my card into the waitress's hand. It shocked the rich family. Unsettled their paradigm. But under all the the posturing and hand wringing and frustration, a glimmer of gratitude lay in the tall grass. Gratitude coy as a tiger strike. It's often asked: what can you get the person who has everything?

The answer?

Any old thing. The son, my friend, once told me he'd kill just to have a brother. To have a corn dog with me. To go berry picking with me and get his hands cut up rather than protected in the comfort of his mansion. He still struggles to let his guard down and belly laugh with me in public. The opposite side of Gatsby's endgame freakout is the rich Vanderbilt who never flinches even when his mother dies. I've since bought meals for architects, finance guys, a millionaire fashion stylist, a billionaire land owner, the list goes on. But also the poor, the destitute.

The reaction is always the same: political and social posturing hides a fragile core of gratitude.

"Least" could, of course, merely mean the *most* hungry (aka: least full). It has grown in vogue to say capitalism has reduced poverty, but check for inflation and you'll find that false. Particularly when you're using absolute poverty metrics rather than relative metrics.

Even with absolute metrics, poverty has not decreased but grown out of control. Dr. Jason Hickel of the London School of Economics points out that yes, the wealthy of the first world give $128 billion in nonprofit aid every year.

But what do the wealthy of the first world take out *before they give that $128 billion?*

1. $60 billion in TRIPS (intellectual property rights internationally — may not seem like an obvious thing, but when you're prevented from building solar panels and your country has never had coal plants… like Central India…)
2. $138 billion in tax holidays
3. $211 billion in interest payments
4. $480 billion in structural adjustments
5. $486 billion in repatriated profits
6. $571 billion in climate change damage
7. $700 billion WTO Uruguay round
8. $973 billion in capital flight from BoP leakages
9. $1.75 trillion in trade misinvoicing and abusive transfer pricing
10. $2.66 trillion in unequal exchange

Which, when subtracted from the $128 billion, leaves us with -$7.9 trillion loss that the global north stole from the global south. Even if you deny all the data that *oil companies themselves publish about climate change in order to accelerate climate change so that more drilling places on the North Slope would emerge,* you still end up with -$7.4 trillion loss that rich countries stole from poor:

> *"What this means is that poor countries are net creditors to rich countries - exactly the opposite of what we would usually assume. But when we consider the aid budget in its broader context, we should look not only at outward flows but also at the losses and costs that developing countries have suffered as a result of policies devised by rich countries. For instance, when structural adjustment was imposed on the global south during the 1980s and 1990s, they lost around $480 billion per year in potential GDP."*
>
> — Dr. Jason Hickel, *The Divide*

At some point, the problem isn't the individual but the collective: at some point you *do* need to assess the structural problems. And not in the Judas way. Judas says the perfume could have been sold and the money given to the poor. Jesus says the poor you will always have with you, *but you will not always have me*: he's quoting Deuteronomy.

"If anyone is poor among your fellow Israelites in any of the towns of the land the Lord your God is giving you, do not be hardhearted or tightfisted toward them. Rather, be openhanded and freely lend them whatever they need. Be careful not to harbor this wicked thought: "The seventh year, the year for canceling debts, is near," so that you do not show ill will toward the needy among your fellow Israelites and give them nothing. They may then appeal to the Lord against you, and you will be found guilty of sin. Give generously to them and do so without a grudging heart; then because of this the Lord your God will bless you in all your work and in everything you put your hand to. There will always be poor people in the land. Therefore I command you to be openhanded toward your fellow Israelites who are poor and needy in your land.

"If any sell themselves to you and serve you six years, in the seventh year you must let them go free. And when you release them, do not send them away empty-handed. Supply them liberally from your flock, your threshing floor and your winepress. Give to them as the Lord your God has blessed you. Remember that you were slaves in Egypt and the Lord your God redeemed you. That is why I give you this command today."
— Deuteronomy 15

Jesus is saying that Judas *had the poor among*. They were already there. He's not offering a cynical, "Well you'll always have poor people, so what's the point of giving?" He's saying *where were you with all the poor we had around us the whole time, Judas?* Judas "didn't say this because he cared about the poor." Jesus says, "But you will not always have me." He's saying *to the apostles* he sold himself as a slave. Who gave back to God-made-slave as slave-made-God has blessed him? Who gave to Jesus mindful of the fact that she, herself, was a slave in Egypt? The prostitute with the nard.

Jesus comes *as the poor*.

It's the rich young ruler who comes to Jesus, right? You know the story. Guy comes to Jesus, has a ton of money and power. Asks Jesus for homework. A mission. "*What is your name? What is your quest?*"

He asks, "What must I do to be saved?"

Jesus says, "You know the commands. You shall not commit adultery. You shall not steal. You shall not give false testimony. Honor your father and mother."

He said, "All these I have kept since I was a boy."

Jesus said, "You still lack one thing: sell everything you have and give it to the poor and you will have treasure in heaven. Then come follow me."

When he heard this, he became very sad, because he was very wealthy. Jesus looked at him and said, "How hard it is for the rich to enter the kingdom of God! Indeed, it is easier for a camel to go through the eye of a needle than for someone who is rich to enter the kingdom of God."

Those who heard this asked, "Who then can be saved?"

Jesus replied, "What is impossible with man is possible with God."

Peter said to him, "We have left all we had to follow you!"

"Truly I tell you," Jesus said to them, "no one who has left home or wife or brothers or sisters or parents or children for the sake of the kingdom of God will fail to receive many times as much in this age, and in the age to come eternal life."

Now.

That gets explained away at virtually every conference and church ever. *"Jesus didn't mean what he said, yada yada yada."* I think he did, and here's the key:

"No one is good except God alone."

God has all of the power, all the money, all the pleasure, all the honor, all the fame, all being, beauty, truth: he *is* Goodness.

From that position, he condescends and gives all. From that position, he takes the lowest place. From such great heights, he divests himself of power and money and revokes fame and honor and sets aside pleasure to become a baby for us.

And thus is really and truly and completely good. God before the rich young ruler.

Here's a man who keeps all the commands. All the rules. He keeps the regulations and tax returns and Robert's Rules of Order and doesn't break taboos with his wife and gets along with the judges at the awards ceremony. Mark adds that Jesus "looked at him and loved him."

Yet this righteous rich young ruler has power and money in a world full of bad things and bad people.

How?

Jesus says no one is Goodness except God.

If the man has that much power and money — enough that such a call to poverty and divestiture makes him this sad, this defensive — then whose fault is it when not he, but the systems he exploits, hurt others?

Whose fault is it that he got money and power from institutions that cheat and betray and rely on state sanctioned murder and exile?

Whose fault is it that his power and money are propped up by a company or government entity's false testimony and legal loopholes?

Whose fault is it that, though he himself honors his father and mother, yet his father and mother suffer dishonor on account of the religious and political and commercial institutions with whom he partners?

He may not covet, but does the company he runs do mergers and acquisitions? Do they try to put their "competition" out of business through corporate consolidation? Do they steal proprietary technology, intellectual property, and imitate patents?

Do they move boundaries, oil leases, mineral rights, commons managed natural resources, so that the few grow rich through the many perishing? So that what was owned by the entire community is now "owned" by a few robber barons?

Do they benefit from disproportionate trade practices?

In that situation, the only way to remain righteous is to take the *action of passion*, revoke, divest, release, let go and let the bounty move to the poor. It's possible for a man, potentially in some perfect world, to become wealthy and powerful while maintaining his integrity. I have my doubts, but it's hypothetically possible. But it's impossible for him to remain so. Absolutely impossible unless he gets rid of it all. That's what God did. And Jesus is the first one to say that the only way for a rich and powerful man to make it into heaven is to divest, revoke, become obscure and chaste and nameless and penniless. Like what it would take for a camel to get through the eye of a needle.

What would it literally take?

A camel must be reduced down to its atomic parts: to the smallest motes of being and then thread through and stitched up literally like the camel shirt John the Baptist wore.

And if the passage's second and third confirmation (Jesus's goodness as God condescended and the camel illustration) isn't enough for you, Peter follows all of this up with "We have left everything to follow you."

And Jesus says Peter will be rewarded with everything resurrected in the kingdom.

The world is hungry not for want of food. The world is hungry for want of people who give to the undeserving hungry from out of their own undeserved bounty. The world isn't hungry because the poor are guaranteed to live among us and, out of despair we resign them to their fate. Rather out of our resignation *from ignoring them whilst they live among us,* the poor are therefore always among us and Jesus is here with them only a little while.

The world is poor not because it has too little, but because dragons hoard too much and need the Lion of Judah to plunder their hoard and carve them out of their scale suit.

Said harsher:

If you're as sad as the rich young ruler, then you're fat or lonely or aching for a job to do because the poor starve and connect and work their heart out. You think, at least according to your nation's policies, that they deserve it. The easiest weight loss program out there — the rosiest cure to loneliness and boredom — is to make it easier for the global south to eat. To decide — today — that you and not social security or some church scholarship will take care of them.

So sell it all and feed the people you think don't deserve it.

Cause the truth is, the more you have the easier it is to make money. Your money makes money. Your bootstraps make bootstraps that pull up still a third set of your bootstraps.

You don't deserve it either. And you know it deep down.

Why?

The poor work harder than you. And you're terrified of being that poor again.

THE EXPOSED.

In that old hippie movie about the life of St. Francis *Brother Sun, Sister Moon*, there's an old friar who shows up late to the monastery naked. St. Francis says, "Why are you naked?"

The friar says, "I gave my robe to a naked beggar."

St. Francis says, "That's good of you. Here's a new one, don't give it away."

He comes back the next night naked.

"What did you do?"

"Another naked beggar. I gave my robe."

St. Francis laughs, gives him a new one. "I *forbid you* to give this one away."

Next night, naked again.

"Brother, what did you do?" St. Francis asks. "I forbade you to give it away."

"I know! I didn't!"

"Then why are you naked?"

"I went up to a naked beggar and said, 'The founder of my order has forbidden me to give away my robe anymore. But if you forcibly take it from me, I will not resist you."

Some deserve to be naked more than others.

Will you give your robe to the undeserving naked?

Perhaps the people who deserve clothes the least in our culture are nudists. They don't want them. Clearly. *Clearly.* I remember a story from Frank O'Pinion on the Big 550 KTRS talk show. My dad used to listen to AM in the PM all the time: an AM radio station for the blue collar guys on the way to their *next* job or headed home late from work. It's not the sort of thing you'll see referenced in any other book like this and, frankly, I can't recommend it on several counts. Frank — or one of his cohosts — apparently did sales in California in an early job. Knocked on the door and a beautiful couple answers. "Hey I'm Frank," he says. "I'm selling the latest whatsit and doohickey."

"You can come in and we can listen," the man said, "there's just one stipulation."

About that time Frank realized both wore nothing but white robes.

"We're nudists so you have to pitch to us naked."

I'll spare you the details, but they involve glass furniture. Frank got the sale. He wasn't selling clothes.

There's a similar kind of guy in New York: a naked cowboy. He's the sort of dude who wears tightie whities, his pectorals, and a guitar in Times Square in the February Blizzard. You ever try to robe such a one?

Our next door neighbor lived across the alley. The designer from 100 years prior had designed our apartments to be wider. Only two per floor, not the current railroad layout of four hundred square feet and four units per floor. Well when you do that and there's an alley of air between you both four stories up, when the windows align four per apartment so that, when curtainless, you can see fifteen feet across into each other's business, you end up with your dining room table facing straight out the window into our neighbor's bathroom. Your kitchen sink ends up across from their couch. I'll spare you hyper specific details again, but you end up facing exhibitionists having a lot of loud naked sex in the screen of the window across the way while you're hosting dinner guests at your own house. You end up with a ton of open doors on their bathroom while you answer emails at your kitchen table. You end up begging God for those folks to get curtains and begging your wife to get them for your kitchen. You end up on a late cool night by yourself in your home working on the computer with the windows open on a dark alley and windows shining light across the way with some exhibitionist shouting back at you, "She's naked! Completely naked!"

You leave after shouting back across the alley, "I did not design this apartment!"

You draw the outline of their apartment and your own in order to show the landlord, whose hands are tied, exactly how this situation developed. But you wish they'd get curtains or clothes.

Sometimes the least of these naked are rather hard to robe. It's like a kid running around nekked like a white tail buck straight out of the bathtub while you're doing your best to chase them with a towel.

Sometimes it's the underdressed. Wandering prophets like me *hate* fashion in any form. We hate preachers in expensive sneakers, fashion week, the

Oscars. Ricky Gervais at the Golden Globes speaks to us. If you're going to have high fashion, you might as well bring back the middle ages where fashion *means* something and folks use it sincerely. And sometimes we need those folks to come alongside us and clothe us when we are unaware of our nakedness or even underclothed willfully.

For me, it was Andrew. Andrew worked as a cinematographer for P Diddy and other folks. On set with stylists all day. He was the kind of dyed-in-the-wool New York Italian that always dressed in various textiles bleached white. He was hot here one summer with us and I said, "You're in long sleeves. Why aren't you as sweaty as me?"

"Linens."

Now I'm an old country boy at heart and I've heard that word in exactly three places: the book of Revelation, my wife whilst dress shopping, and bedsheets. Never in my life had I heard another man use the word "linens." But, willfully underdressed as I am, I bought a $20 shirt on sale midsummer in Brooklyn. 103°F with thick humidity like the air itself had over-exerted itself. I went out in it, nothing but new linen, and for the first time in seven years I, the undeserving underdressed, had sweat through a shirt only to walk into the shade and feel the breeze turn my overheated body into a fridge. Beyond cooling me down, the shirt *dried*.

Andrew died of a heart attack that year, this time on the film set of his dreams, using a script he had written with his new bride. I have no doubt he died well dressed. And I remain grateful for his generosity in having clothed me.

It's true that sometimes "least" simply means most vulnerable in a category. Certainly naked children fit here: vulnerable to elements and vulnerable to abuse. It's these of whom Jesus said it would be better to have a millstone around your neck and thrown into the sea than to let them come to harm. Clothing the naked, in this instance, is more than clothes and more a systematic approach to keeping naked, vulnerable children from being abused in their nakedness. Better books, more targeted books, have been written about that. Seek them out if you're in a leadership position over kids, for all that is good and holy. The guide that almost every organization bases their teaching and policies off of comes from the United States Conference of Catholic Bishops in their child and youth protection section:

https://www.usccb.org/offices/child-and-youth-protection/diocesan-resources

Why do organizations across denominations and secular sectors of society use that guide? Because the Catholic church botched this issue so publicly, so horribly that an organization bent towards self-correction (historically) *had* to learn how to fix the problem. Their own journalists and lawyers forced them to do so. Julie Ann Smith runs a blog called *Defend the Sheep*. Doug Lay's also a great contact, former missionary who himself faced abused and has helped many others.

When you say you want to go into full-time ministry, you think this means weekly sermons and you do not think this means climbing into a bathtub naked with a wolf.

This is not a metaphor.

One of our neighbors here — a young friend — was practically dying.

She was very, very ill and I was very, very worried for her.

We didn't know how to help her and then Tara suggested I walk her "dog." Her "dog" has a foot-long snout and "the better to see you with" eyes and "the better to eat you with" teeth. Her "dog" is a wolf from one of the few wolf rescues in the U.S.

Not a wolf-dog. A wolf. 99.9% American Greywolf. As in Little Red Riding Hood and the… As in The Three Little Pigs and the… As in Peter and the… This wolf sometimes poses for high-dollar photo shoots with actors like Kit Harrington for… *The North remembers* reasons. Ghost. And Jon Snow.

I later found out he had once bit into a dog watcher's arm twice and gave puncture wounds two to three inches deep all up the guy's forearm. Deep, deep wounds that required serious layered stitches. In two bites. Cause he felt irritated.

The wolf has to go on mile-and-a-half-long walks to even get ready to poo. As in thirty blocks. I have to keep him on a six-inch leash because of how strong he is. Often I had to literally belay his leash around my entire body as if he's a mountain climber and I'm the guy trying to create a counterweight to save him — or some innocent bystander — from certain death.

The walks went okay. He had freaked out a bit, but he was doing okay. Then Tara and I showed up later in the day and he'd crapped and peed all over his cage and literally flung it all over this really nice Persian rug she has. I have no idea how he flung it. Maybe with his feet. Maybe his teeth, who knows?

Did I mention that wolves are smarter than dogs?

Because they are.

This wolf knew *exactly* what he had done, mad to be crated.

He wanted out, regardless of whether or not mom had grown sick to the edge of dying.

Tara offered to steam the rug and clean the house while I took him to the doggie car wash. In New York, they have these places where you can shampoo your dog the same way you shampoo your car. A cattle stall.

Walked twenty blocks. He went number one and number two. Number two had bones in it. Large bones. Because he eats raw porterhouse steaks. Can you see how this becomes a mind game between me and the wolf? The first self-wash was open. The wolf recognized it and started yanking me around the store and flailing and digging in his back paws. Turned out their self-service stopped at 4:30pm. Tried to go uptown, but that one had closed. We walked another twenty blocks west to the place near Washington Square, closed at 5:30pm. It's 7pm. I text the girls: No go, all closed. We're up five miles of forced marching.

The wolf's mother texts back:

I guess bathtub it is :o

Now.

Texting and driving is bad. Texting and maintaining your alpha status as leader of a wolf pack is worse. That last text was the last straw and the wolf freaked out. He started jumping up like a kingfisher, he grabbed the leash in his jaws and yanked harder than a marlin, he jumped up — when fully extended on his hind legs, he's much taller than me — and scratched me. I'm wearing my nice herringbone jacket. He bites my left bicep and tricep. Not to kill, but the way he'd bite a pack member he intends to challenge. The arm bruise went all green and tennis-ball sized the next day. There's still a hole in my jacket.

I didn't know what else to do. None of the posturing worked. None of the leash snapping worked. The more I fought him, the more he fought me. Large crowds on the East Village sidewalk started giving us both a wide berth. I grew very, very afraid.

He smelled the fear.

So I tapped into my flight response, shouted, "COME! LESSGO!" and took off at a dash down the sidewalk. He yanked at me for awhile and then he went into his slow gallop. For the record, I used to be a 100-meter dasher and 300-hurdles sprinter. I used to play wide receiver. I used to be the guy in baseball who'd get on first base every time, but couldn't hit a home run. I'm a fast dude when I want to be.

I was going full speed and he was barely jogging. Wasn't even winded. That was the most terrifying thing: had I desperately wanted to in an emergency, I would never, ever outrun this wolf. He would *drag me to hell and back* if he wanted *while* I sprinted.

We got back to the place and his mom had me tie him to the stairwell bannister while we clean up. She's to the point where she's getting winded from laughing, from walking up a couple of flights of stairs. She went to bed for a bit and I started scrubbing wolf droppings off the massive crate in the bathtub with a pitcher. Tara steam cleaned a 100-square-foot rug and another one that ran the length of the hall. We did dishes and things, scrubbed and scrubbed while mom rested.

After an hour or so, I asked his mom how best to do it.

"You're going to have to get naked with him," she said.

"Okay," I said.

NARRATOR: It was not okay.

"If you put him into the bathtub and stay clothed, he'll think you're doing something *to* him. If you get in first, he'll want to join the pack and will just come right in with you."

"Naked with the wolf," I said. "Got it. Any advice? Use the showerhead?"

"At first," she said. "You'll have to get him to stand to get his belly. Use the rose shampoo. I figure if we have to do it he might as well come out smelling like roses."

"Smell like roses, okay. Anything else?"

"Make sure the shower door handle is on the side next to the toilet and the showerhead. If it's on the backside of the tub, he'll make a mess of things."

"How so?"

"He'll climb out."

"Of the *shower*?"

"Yes," she said. She whispered over the goiter.

"Like over *the entire shower wall*?"

"Yes."

She waited in bed as I went around the hall and stared at the wolf.

I closed the baby gate made for baby tree ents. Hilarious, in retrospect. I went to get the wolf. He saw me and lifted his leg and peed all over the stairs in the hallway. It ran down several flights. He was trying to prove a point.

I went and got paper towels and started cleaning, refusing to untie him. He tried gnawing on me to get me to untie him. I refused and I eventually dodged him enough to get it all cleaned up.

Then I turned him loose and got him into the bathroom and closed the door.

I became painfully aware that I was inside a six-foot-by-six-foot cell with a full grown wolf.

THIS IS NOT WHAT I HAD IN MIND WHEN I WENT TO OZARK CHRISTIAN COLLEGE WHO PROMISED TO TRAIN ME FOR CHRISTIAN SERVICE.

Normally my dog freaks out at this part in the bath. The wolf didn't. He just started being ornery, climbing onto the sink and biting cleaning supplies and tongue scrapers and tubes of toothpaste and metal utensils. I got it all out of him and off of him and away from him and I tried not to draw his attention to the clothes I was taking off because he really likes ripping fabric. I got down to my skivvies and I prayed the prayer Saint Francis prayed, aloud, right into the eyes of this thing:

"Brother Wolf, God made you beautiful and wily, fast and strong. I pray you be tender with me as I pass."

Then naked, the boy entered the shower and turned on the shower head.

Ladies and gentlemen, the wolf has entered the arena.

I started to sing in order to calm him and closed the door slowly behind, his three-foot-long tail slipping inside.

And then, there in the water, the boy died and the man was born. I've heard of rites of passage, but this was surreal. I mean, I wouldn't have considered myself a boy or even necessarily a coward — I'm thirty at the time, for crying out loud — but there's something about tearing off all of your armor and then stepping into the waters with the wolf and then washing him, slowly, of all the crap he'd rubbed all over himself… the slow cleansing ritual soothed my spirit as much as cleaning up the older gentlemen and older ladies in the hospital used to sooth my spirit. But the older folk couldn't kill me. You never stop on an orthopedic floor and think, *Could I take this ninety year old woman with a broken hip in a fistfight?* There was this deep respect and honor involved as well, as if I needed to bow in courtesy and chilvary before shampooing the monster. It took a ton of water. We were in there for half an age of men. He drank a good deal of it (which meant he'd throw up in his crate twice later and we'd need to clean that up again too). I got pretty scratched up when I got him to stand on my naked chest and wash his naked belly and he got some twelve bottles down from the very high ledge and into the standing water, demolishing one of the bottle caps, gushing expensive stuff that smelled of hippie incense.

But through changes various, through all vicissitudes, we made our way.

We drained it. I got out and used one towel to distract him while shouting, "TORO! TORO!" and the other to dry him. He shredded the first towel. He took three of my towels off my naked body in succession and got very, very curious with my pants. I would have to ride the subway home commando, but…

The naked wolf was clean. And the naked wolf was dry. His coat was restored.

And the Lancelot was not dead yet.

He peed his cage afterwards. Puked. We cleaned it up before he got it all over again, I walked him a second time, and then it was okay. We ate dinner and I read a chapter of my novel and made the mom with the goiter laugh and then she went to bed too after rhubarb pie and kombucha and a prayer.

Walking back to the subway, Tara and I just started laughing and couldn't stop.

"Our life is absurd," I said.

"Wouldn't have it any other way."

"How's my hole?" I asked, pointing to the jacket.

She giggled. "Fine. Now you can say a wolf tried to eat it." This, my homeschooled bride.

All told, it took seven and a half hours — 5pm to 12:30am. The trains were running local. We got to bed at 2 in the morning.

The boy was dead.

The man was born.

And he grew and became strong, was filled with wisdom and stature and the grace of God was upon him…

A week later, our friend grew worse. She needed us to walk the wolf and grab about sixty pounds of porterhouse steaks. Because he eats raw meat.

I won't tell you about that trip.

I'll tell you about when we came back and asked to pray over the goiter in her neck:

So a minister said she would take care of me. Of course. I feel like I have shaken off my old life and one by one the only ones who come are the ones with faith.

I think that's true, I texted back.

When you both were praying I saw a golden light and then silver and my thyroid is much smaller.

That's awesome, I texted back. Thanks to Jesus for that. We ask for the goiter to decrease more. I'm praying when you wake up it's back to normal.

It worked. I'm so humbled and grateful.

He likes you a lot, I texted. Dances over you, even. I'm glad he showed you in this way.

I was just giving thanks for the both of you, feeling the energy coming off you.

I'm grateful you feel much better. Still praying it increases until you see total healing and feel whole.

Amen brother. Love you Tara.

Sometimes the wolf deserves to be naked. Filthy. Unclothed. And sometimes you climb into the tub anyways — if for nothing else, because it will make you better.

Another time, I went to a conference and an older friend, a woman, was riding with me and another coordinator as we took her to the airport. I'm being intentionally vague here for the sake of her privacy, but she had a ton of fluids and we got stuck in traffic. I think the nerves got to her before the flight, but it made her really, really have to go and she thought she'd pee her pants in the SUV. Now in that situation, I've met fathers who have said to kids, "It's your own fault, just pee your pants and we will clean it out when we get there." But luckily for her, I had had another experience like this on the road in the desert.

In high school, we had gone to a native American reservation to pour concrete and build some stuff and paint. And between sights in the Arizona desert, there lie long stretches of highway without any respite. Halfway down one of those stretches a buddy of mine had to poop. He told the driver, but word spread through the fifteen passenger van. He had to go, they said. There's no where to go, they said.

"I'll drive as fast as I can, but you're going to have to hold it for about an hour," Jeff, the driver, said.

"Okay, I'll try."

So passed the quietest hour I've ever encountered in a van full of awake chaperones and students. And it never passed in full. Halfway through, my buddy started sweating. He said, "Oh. Oh no. Oh no oh no oh no. Please. Please no. *Please nooooo.*"

A smell filled the car.

"It's too late."

We rode in silence with the windows down until he could get his change of clothing.

That's what I had in mind when my elder colleague said she had to pee — that she would pee her pants on the way to the airport. The driver looked everywhere for a bathroom but we had gridlock traffic. I mean we weren't moving at all. So she decided to hop out and squat over in the corner by the chain link while the cars sat. It was nearing winter and cold. I had my grey trench coat. I turned my head and made her as big of a curtain as I could muster with the trench coat while the cars passed. She finished. We hopped back in the car and went off.

There are two ways to respond to the undeserving naked: one is to tell them to *hold it*, it's your own fault, just change your pants when you get there.

The other is this: hold up your trench coat to the undeserving naked so they can get a little dignity back. Bathe the crap-covered wolf. Even if it means *you* have to strip down naked for them to be clothed.

Even if the naked forcibly take your robes, do not resist them.

THE DEHYDRATED.

The following two chapters from my novel *Bell Hammers* grew out of interviews from my grandfathers. As far as I can confirm historically, what follows is pretty much how it happened. The first chapter, I should note, originally sold to *The New Haven Review*, of Yale's Institute Library. It tells the story of why my grandfather thirsted.

Wilson Remus
1958

"I like the other one," she said.

"But it's so heavy," Remmy said.

"I know. I like a sturdy table," she said.

"There's kitchen tables and then there's butcher's blocks. I don't plan on slaughtering a hog in my dining room."

"I might," she said. "I'm the cook, don't forget."

Remmy sighed. "Do you think it's pretty?"

"I do."

"Do you think anyone else will?"

"What do I care for what anyone else thinks?"

"I'm not going to answer that question, you'll get me into trouble no matter which way I go."

"Wilson Remus Broganer, what's that supposed to mean?"

Wilson Remus Broganer said nothing to his pregnant wife.

"Well in any case," she said, "I like it and I think it matches everything else so this is what we're getting."

"All right now, I didn't mean to make you mad."

"I'm not mad. I'm decisive."

"And you won yourself a decisive victory. Okay now, let's get it to the bag checker."

"They don't make bags big enough for this, honey."

"You know what I mean." He hefted the massive slab of wood. "You know what I mean," he muttered as he grunted and hefted it over to one of the counters with one of them Sears and Roebuck signs and they bought it and, with much struggle, took it home.

"Five dollars a month," he kept mumbling as he drove. "Five dollars a month. I could buy a share of Texarco at the end of the year."

"Well then, let's take it back."

"You were listening to me?"

"You weren't whispering, really, now were you?"

"I meant to be."

"You didn't mean very well."

He harrumphed. "Well, I'm glad you have your table."

"Are you?"

"It's just so big."

"I think it's pretty."

And so they went until they got home. He set up the table, and it filled that room as does the king's table in a great hall. Except this was no castle. Not quite yet.

But once he saw it in place, he was pleased enough with it.

"You're smiling," she said.

"It's a pretty table set up like that."

"That's why I made you buy it."

"I just did a good job setting it up."

She did not return the affirmation.

Two weeks later, the biggest and baddest tornado any of them carpenters could remember hit. It snapped hundred-year-old trees in two. It leveled some houses and frayed some power lines.

When it hit, Remmy was at home with Beth.

"It's a semi-hurricane!" Beth screamed.

"Tornado."

"We're going to die!"

"We might," Remmy said.

"Why would you say such a thing?"

"I mean I'm sure we'll be fine honey. Let's go to the storm shelter."

Well they went outside and that wind blew everything. Tore at the trees. Tore at the roof he'd just fixed up. There were boards and water thrown every which way. Beth waddled a bit with her swollen body and the baby inside. They got to the storm shelter door that Remmy had just dug and they opened it up and damned if there wasn't two feet of water down there.

"That's not a storm shelter," Beth said.

"Sure it is, get inside!"

"That's a pool! That's an underground lake like in the movies where the monsters hide, I'm not going down in there!"

They were shouting over the wind, mind you. Stuff still blowing all around them.

"You get in there or I'll get you in there," he said. "We're not going back in that house! I know how it's made, remember!"

"You do whatever you want," she said, "but me and the baby are going back inside."

He watched her go, holding that sheet metal door like he was. Then he groaned and let it slam and he barely heard it over the cry of the train rumbling in the sky. He started following her inside and then he shouted to no one in particular, "Where on earth'd my brand new lawn chairs go?" They'd been metal chairs, heavy chairs, sturdy chairs, and not a one of them was in the backyard.

Back in the house, Beth was pacing, slowly, off-kilter. "What do we do?"

"You vetoed my plan!"

"What do we do? What do we do?"

The house had been built just on concrete blocks. Well the wind got under there like two stock boys will get under a box and it lifted the whole house up about six inches and slammed it back down again.

Beth screamed.

Remmy, for once, had nothing to say.

"What do we do?" She was begging, now.

The house was lifted higher and slammed down on those concrete blocks again. Some plaster fell off the ceiling in the other room.

The table.

Remmy went into action. "You get under there. It's new but it's the strongest thing we've got."

She got under there, moving like a station wagon with two missized wheels, like a wheel with a ten pound weight on one wall. Then she sat still and some plaster fell off the ceiling and onto that five-dollar a month Sears and Roebuck kitchen table.

Remmy didn't bother to duck under anything but one of the open doorframes, leaning against it like some cowboy watching his horse from the porch of a saloon. "Five dollars a month. Decent insurance policy, I guess, I don't know."

More plaster fell.

The house bounced once or twice more. Then the wind died down.

And then a sound like what you'd expect if Chicken Little'd been right and the sky really did fall. Something like the crashing of the Tower of Babel. Something like the fall of Troy or the breaching of Atlantis's levy.

Finally, all went calm. He walked outside.

There stretched out in his yard, discarded as if some god of greed had found no more fun in a playtoy, sat a massive tower. As if the angels had gotten bored with their scaffolding for building the pearly gates and had kicked it over the edge of heaven.

"Bethy come look! Come look, it's awful! It's an awesome thing to look at."

The neighbor carpenters and their families were outside too on their front porches, looking at the mangled black thing spread across the yards, the rain still coming down and none of them caring, not even the prettier ones in their nightgowns a bit too early—maybe his neighbor Joe'd been weathering the storm with a little bit of marital duty. How people do cling to one another in hard times, even if it ends up with your neighbor Joe's wife standing half naked on her porch.

Beth came out and looked with Remmy. They all looked at one another.

Then they all stared at the massive steel oil derrick, as long as a water tower is tall. His father'd told him about these things, about how they drilled with big old bits. And about the salt water tank at the top. He looked at the top. It had cracked on impact, and the great salt water tower was bleeding out over all of their yards. That, along with the rain, was turning the ditches and divots to estuaries. Some of the neighbor kids ran out and played in it.

But all Remmy could think about was that salt. All of that salt. Right on top of their wells. He stared at it, his eyes staring at the eye in the tower where the... well it might as well have been where the poison came out.

Beth cried out behind him. He turned and found her clutching her belly and leaking some water of her own, the cramps of early labor scared into her from the crashing and banging about.

He swore.

"Don't swear!" she yelled. "This is a blessing!"

"Not in the rain and the wet!"

She screamed. Oh, how she cried out from the pain.

The neighbor ladies came. Beth went inside with them. Remmy fretted and occupied himself with the boys. They went over to the tower to try to stop the bleeding, but the crack widened, rimmed with white, and the water kept on coming. Some of the younger men actually tried to put their hands on the thing, which was about like trying to stop Niagara with your shoulder or some such stupidity.

While they were working over in Joe's yard, they found Remmy's white metal table and chairs in a hedgerow, now dirty from all the mud and sewage that'd slung about in the wind.

"New chairs!" said Joe.

"Like hell!"

"Oh come on, Remmy, finders keepers. Those are nice lawn chairs."

"Well in that case," Remmy said, "I just found this house sitting out here after the storm." He pointed to Joe's house.

"Oh, I was only joking."

"Well joke these over into my yard with me, will ya?"

They hauled them.

"You know," Joe said as they walked back into Remmy's yard, "I heard they got the name derrick from a hangman in England."

"Come on, now."

"That's what I heard. Cause they call cranes derricks too. Big towers to hang things from, you know, like a hangman and his noose. Sticking out over to stick something down into a hole like that."

"I'll be damned. Derrick the hangman. It makes sense, I guess."

They never did get the hole plugged. Not with wood. Not with clay or plaster or the pig carcass one of the boys tried. Where he got it, nobody asked because some things just were. After several hours of this, the women came back out and told him he had a son. He ran in to find Beth there, tired and smiling, in the middle of more blood than he was comfortable seeing. The blood there reminded him of a full bottle of ketchup he'd watched get accidentally shattered while he was flirting with some girl at a diner as a teenager, tomato blood scattering all over. But he smiled all the same because he had a son. He named him Tobias—Toby.

Three weeks later, Toby died of pneumonia. It must have been the rain and the wet.

That was the year the Army Corps of Engineers started damming the Kaskaskia River to make Carlyle Lake. Through eminent domain, the government bought out house after house of the townships in the river valley. They capped sixty-nine oil wells.

They exhumed some six hundred graves, some of them undoubtedly holding the remains of ancestors of Native Americans as well as the remains of babies.

Wilson Remus
1959

Had that boy who tried to stuff the pig carcass into the hole in that fallen oil derrick succeeded, had the neighbor men succeeded in plugging it with that clay or their shoulders the day heaven spat out that great black tower in the tornado, it would have saved Remmy a good stroke of trouble.

The first thing that oily recycled saltwater from its top tank did was get into the fishing lake nearby—the end point of all the ditches and culverts. Water seeks the lower place, you see, and this explains all rivers and ditches and salt water runoffs from oil derricks that fall from heaven. The fish in the lake died within the week. Then the turtles and snakes followed — the ones that didn't leave, the ones that stuck around. The men who ate the fish got sick. The merry men took to calling the lake The Dead Sea.

Remmy didn't eat the fish. Wouldn't let Beth eat the fish. In the year that followed the whole tornado event, Beth got pregnant again and had what everyone called their first child — a daughter named Marionette who was born in the oil fields when Beth went to bring John David a lunchbox. Remmy didn't curse his dad but he did curse: he was afraid of another incident like Toby's pneumonia. He didn't want his second child to die a week into life and every time he heard anyone call Marionette his first child, he'd get somber and say, "I had a son. His name was Toby," and he'd go off in the corner and drink or go outside and look up at the night sky and pray for a shooting star. He did even when he got old, and it was a sad thing to see.

But he couldn't have that rest right now, looking as he was at the land and the indented spot where the oil derrick had sat on their front yards. Not that Texarco had hauled it off. Texarco didn't settle on the damage done and didn't even seem to want their derrick back. No, what had happened after it had drained out all of its nastiness and no one had come to claim it was this:

Remmy'd rallied all them carpenters together and he'd gotten ahold of Pete Taylor and some others too and they all sat around waiting for him to speak. Pete Taylor nodded at Remmy once Ryan and Sinclair and Bullhorn and all of them'd shown up. Remmy told them that if no one was going to claim it then they were gonna claim all that metal for themselves, and to get their wrenches and flatbeds and whatnot and they'd work all night if they had too.

Well they did, they worked all of them — all experts in handmade demolition — tearing that oil derrick down into the braces and bolts and things all night long. And Remmy worked up a deal where they'd all buy a shed out west of Bellhammer, closer to Carlyle where he had half a mind to move. Well it wasn't really a shed, it was a warehouse, but they put all of those parts of that tower in there and built up the nicest shelves any warehouse had, repainted them a darker shade of black, and stored all their building supplies and tools in there for a good long while until they'd figure out something better to do with it.

After the shed and that crummy old house, Remmy'd spent his whole savings fund, but that's what they'd done with the derrick anyways and all the men and all their families swore themselves to a solemn oath of secrecy, and since all of them paid for the warehouse, all of them had red on their hands, so to speak. That's how it worked in those days: there were some things you didn't keep no record of because it wasn't worth telling the whole world what you knew more than it was worth watching over the few who were in on it. For instance if you knew the hiding place for the bones of The Great Black Tower.

Remmy thought on this as they hauled it off, sitting drinking a Miller from the comfort of the white metal lawn chair he'd retrieved from Joe's hedgerow after the storm. He'd cleaned it off with the hosepipe.

He couldn't rest from his labors in the company of those he loved. Not yet. He'd have to settle for working in the company of those he loved. And they needed a well, badly. He'd been hauling water from Carlyle every week after the derrick, but it was getting old, so he decided to go to Jim Johnstone, the main boss for that region of Texarco's oil fields.

Remmy walked into this guy's office. It was one of those cheap standing buildings men like that have erected out in the middle of a big project rather than some fancy office building. His fancy office building was back at Texarco's HQ. This was his war tent for the battlefield. It would be left behind like bones of his fallen foes. They had one of those chest-high receiving counters made of speckled white particle board. And also faux-wood panel walls, just to give it a touch of class, Remmy guessed.

"Good morning James," he said. He had decided not to call him 'Jim.'

"Good morning Remmy. How's your father?"

"Working the fields for all I know."

"Mmm." Jim didn't bother to look up at Remmy, just smoked his corncob pipe. Had probably forty of them, one for every pipe tobacco he smoked, treating them like they'd been hewn and whittled by Sacajawea herself, even though they were nothing but stupid old smelly corncob pipes.

Remmy said, "James…"

James snapped awake and looked up at Wilson Remus Broganer.

"That oil derrick landed on my yard."

"Oh do not tell me it's still there," James said. "I told those—"

"No no." He thought about lying about it, but the Good Lord told him, "Don't you lie to him, Remmy, or you'll be as bad as him."

So Remmy didn't say anything more than, "No, the derrick's gone."

"Oh," Jim said. "Well then what's the problem?"

"There was a hole busted into it in the storm."

"As it's our property, you need not be worrying about any damage done to the derrick."

Remmy laughed. "That's sweet of you, James Johnstone. You realize that derrick leaked that oily saltwater all over our lands?"

"You lived off that pond?"

"It's a lake."

"You live off of the fish in it?"

"Well, no."

"What's the problem?" The man leaned back in his chair. "I hate fishing anyways. You like to fish?"

48

"Once in awhile, not all that often."

"Well then here's something we can hate together from the comfort of our chairs. Have a smoke with me, Remmy."

"James, I don't care about fish and lakes, though I suppose I should. I care right now about the truth of the matter which is this: your oil derrick ruined and contaminated and adulterated and… and befouled our water supply. All our wells." Remmy was proud of the words he'd come up with. He'd always read more than Daddy John and tried his best to write down new words in the back of all them books.

James was still nodding.

"Well?"

"I don't know what to tell you, Remmy, I'm sorry for your loss, I guess."

"Jim, I want you to pay to put in another well at my house."

"Now Remmy, that's just crazy. That's just crazy asking us to pay for the aftermath of an act of God."

"The Good Lord didn't have nothing to do with the loss of my son, and he did not have anything to do with building no black tower that sticks out its rod to rape the earth."

"Now Remmy, that's not a very nice way to talk about the company that gives your daddy a pension and gives you a chance to build houses for people who keep flocking to Southern Illinois, is it?"

"It's pronounced Illinois."

"Well however it's sounded out," Jim said, "is that a nice way to talk to your employer?"

"Maybe it is and maybe it ain't."

"I think a little bit of gratitude is in order."

"All right then, thank you for giving me, in a roundabout way, a chance to work about a years's worth of income. But I just bought a house from you that's several years worth of income, and without a well, that means you took more than you gave."

James didn't like that. "Terry?"

His secretary perked up.

"Call Brooks and throw this man out. I am not paying to dig him a well."

"I'll show myself out," Remmy said, and he did, and went home.

By that point, everything around The Dead Sea had died — the trees, the grass, and every once in awhile a small rodent like a brown squirrel or a chipmunk. Some of the neighbor kids found a dead badger at one point and carved out its claws and turned them into weaponry.

Remmy asked his father how to drill a well and found out some. He asked some of the boys how to do it, and found out more. He asked this hermit widower farmer out on the edges of the county — guy the kids called a wizard and storyweaver and wombrover who witched wells – and found some stuff he wasn't sure he trusted, but you never know. He read up in the big city library in town. He even called the University of Illinois and they sent him some papers on how to lay bricks up to keep ground water from spilling over, how to make a concrete lid for it, how to protect his own water asset. Their term.

He did it all. Used every last bit of sense he'd found. He witched it and then he borrowed an auger from Kipsy, the guy that normally did these things for people. Kipsy had a couple and said it was okay for Remmy to use it as long as he didn't break it. After that, Remmy rounded up some nice redbrick — a big old pile of it that he stacked neatly next to the house when the time came to put the finishing touches on his — Remmy Broganer's — well.

With that auger, you know, you couldn't start out with a twenty-foot-tall drill bit, you know, else how would you get the leverage to put it in the ground? No, you started with one extension rod, and you could drill down two feet deep. Remmy had a long black power cord stretching from the house like a blacksnake come to watch him, and he leaned over and drilled that two feet. And when he got the two feet and wanted to go deeper, he had to pull it out, pick up a piece of pipe, and add it to extend the drill bit and then drill again a little deeper. Then you'd pull it out again, add another two-foot extender and drill a little deeper. And he did this all into the evening after work, down and down, adding extensions and extensions. And when he hit water it came right up the hole. He tasted it.

Salt water. He pulled out the extensions one at a time, wrapped up the auger, recoiled the blacksnake powercord and went in to bed.

"How did it go honey?"

"I hit saltwater," he said.

"Shucks," she said.

"Yeah, that too."

The next day, after wearing out his arm hammering studs together, he went back to the auger at the opposite end of the yard. He dug down two, four, eight, sixteen, almost thirty feet and hit water again that night and he smiled. He tasted it and tasted its brackishness and swore some more and would have thrown the auger if it wasn't Kipsy's tool. Taking it apart had a soothing effect on him, or at least created a little buffer where he could calm down before going in to Beth. He stacked it up and coiled the cord and went inside.

"Did you get it?" she asked. Marionette cooed over in the corner somewhere.

"I got a hole, if that's what you mean."

"No water?"

"Oh I found water too."

"Oh good!"

"Saltwater."

"Oh Remmy, I'm sorry."

"Love you," he said and kissed her forehead. He walked over and tickled Marionette, who giggled and giggled. As far as I know, that's the last time he tickled her — got too busy to think about it.

He hauled water in the morning and a couple of days later he tried again for a third well, which turned out to be salt. And a fourth. And a fifth.

After six wells, Remmy gave up on the auger and spent a day giving it back to Kipsy.

"Go well?" Kipsy asked him.

He laughed a dark laugh. "Funny old turn of phrase, that."

"Did it?"

"No, but I thank you all the same."

"Need help with it? I can show you how to use it."

Remmy was not insulted because Kipsy didn't mean offense, but it still hurt a little bit, the truth of it. "I worked it okay, thanks Kipsy. Just hit saltwater every time."

"You're pulling my leg."

"Wish that I was."

"In that whole big yard of yours?"

"So far," he said. "So far."

"What are you going to do, Remmy?"

"I'm gonna try a dug well next week."

Putting in a dug well with a short-handled shovel was not the best way to go about it, but it was the only way he had at the time and all he had energy for, which was a fine joke on him since the short-handled shovel ended up taking more energy from him than had he gone hunting for the other kind. But anyways he went to digging and had himself a hole six foot across and he was pulling up the dirt and the mud and slinging it up and up and went through a softer and softer soil, which he did not expect, but he kept going deeper, digging down into the soul of the place to find if it too had been corrupted.

At around fourteen foot deep, he drove his shovel down and got into the sand. He got excited then, as if he'd dug through from Illinois and ended up on the riverbanks of Korea.

He went into the sand all the way, laying up shovelful after shovelful until it piled up outside the hole. He threw that shovel one more time into the sand and the earth swallowed it clear up to the handle. He'd hit good water, he felt sure of it.

Boy, did he ever hit it.

It came up quicker than oil, quicker than anything his father John David had ever seen working in the fields and the derricks. Gushing.

He speared that short-handled shovel up and out of the well he'd dug and he started scrambling up the wall of the well and ran over to the pile of bricks and he loaded them up in that old wheelbarrow and brought them over and dumped them out and mixed him up some mortar as quick as he could and started laying the brick and laying the brick in a great big old circle, the well from every storybook, its cup runneth over. And no matter how fast he laid the brick to line the well, he couldn't beat the flow of the water, the water line beating the height of the liner over and again, so he called up one of Texarco's tank trunks to put its hose in there, which they were happy to do, taking free water, and that tank truck pumped it out as he laid in brick.

But still he couldn't lay brick fast enough. He laid about as best as he could in the water there until he had it laid up six feet off the ground just like the University of Illinois said to. He did it just so and knew he would not get surface water in there. He had ten feet of well, he did. And he set some boards down in there. He poured a concrete top and fitted it to the top. Then he put a stepping box next to it. He bought a pipe big enough to get the stuff out, you know, to get the pump out of the ground so he could get to the water when he wanted.

He got it really nice. And after he'd done all of that, he took a glass and scooped some out and tasted it and it quenched his thirst. Then he scooped himself another glass and took it on into the sanitation department.

"Morning Remmy."

Remmy was smiling. "Morning Tom."

"What you got for me, another test?"

"I do, Tom. I did a dug well this time, built it up really nice."

"Oh that's good, Remmy, that's so good. I was worried about you." He took the glass and ran the tester. "How's your daughter?"

"Getting big. Getting pretty. I'll be beating off the boys with a four-by-four soon enough."

"Well good luck with that." Tom looked down at the test and tsked. "That's got enough salt in it, you could float an egg."

"HORSE MANUER AND APPLEBUTTER!" Remmy loaded what he had with the test up into his car, and he drove back out to the oil fields. He smelled that smell of a sewage or sulfur line filling up the land. Silt and sod. Good soil is really just good crap that's had enough time to mellow out, and in a land covered in rivers and held up by oil wells, the smell of sulfuric crap's high and low and near and far and wide in an oil field. Remmy walked right up to that makeshift Texarco office and opened the door so fast — it was an outward-swinging door — that it hit off the outside and bounced back to slam shut behind him. He cleared that chest-high countertop and jumped over the desk, too, and had that lazy Jim Johnstone up by the collar before the man could finish his shout.

"Leave him alone. Don't be starting a fight," The Good Lord said to him.

"I want a well," he said to The Good Lord.

Jim answered something tepid, but Remmy wasn't listening to that fool. He was listening to The Good Lord.

"I will give you Water," The Good Lord said to him.

"Okay, then," Remmy said.

Jim Johnstone thought Remmy had said Okay to him, had agreed to whatever pissedpants deal he'd struck up in the moment. Remmy left. But he must have scared Jim anyways, which was not a bad thing on general principles.

Remmy went into town and filled out paperwork to start building a house in Carlyle on the lake, near water. And in the woods. Like Robin Hood. Perfect place to finally rest in the company of those he loved. He came back to his house that night and talked to some of the boys about his plan and they liked it and got finally why he'd wanted The Shed where he'd wanted it. But they didn't like his tone about The

Woods. The plan got back to Jim by the next day, and then Jim's reaction got back to Remmy:

"Well that's a good thing," Jim had said to his troops and his boss, "because I think I was just about ready to settle with him. That man had blood in his eyes. I would have given him anything. I'm glad he's out of here — sooner the better."

When he heard this, Remmy said to his neighbors, "Well I probably should have gotten an attorney, but it's over and done with now, and we'll have a lakehouse and all the living water we want."

Beth couldn't be happier, of course. She could buy more tables.

That wasn't before he washed the car twice with that salt water, though. Twice was all it took to corrode that chrome bumper to rust. Imagine had they drunk it.

Perhaps my grandfather and the entire community did not deserve it. Perhaps they came to work for the oil company like Grandma Beth's daddy and those oil people got what they deserved — certainly the narrative of *Bell Hammers* would imply so.

But then again, thirst is terrible. A terrible way to go. Have you ever run an engine without oil? Without a radiator?

You know who doesn't deserve water?

Water thieves like Nestle and the Michigan governor who sold out — who still sells out — the people of Flint. We visited Flint in the fall of 2021 on the way home from a family vacation and it stood out as the starkest part of that trip: the city reminded me of some of the things we've seen in Tunisia and war torn countries. It's devastated by water thieves.

Water polluters like the Keystone Pipeline's war on the native water protectors — same war they've fought on the same land since Wounded Knee.

Water neglecters like every alcoholic you've ever known.

Whoever drinks the water I give them will never thirst.

Perhaps they're thirsty for the wrong thing?

THOSE WITH PREEXISTING CONDITIONS.

The first thing they told me on the way to see Don was that some thought he didn't deserve to live. He'd done it to himself. He had been selfish. Don was a type one diabetic who had drunk and smoked himself into an infection. If you know anything about diabetics, you know an internal infection is about the worst case scenario. I'm married to one (a type one diabetic, not to a worst case scenario, what do you take me for?). Visions of infections dance in my head.

He'd been in and out of the hospital during COVID. Lost a leg. And for three weeks prior to my seeing him, he'd had an infection and almost no one had come to visit. Including his kids.

By the world's standards, here's a washed up apex predator. Here's a man past his prime. Here's an inconvenience in my work day. Here's a burden on the healthcare or social status or family values system. Here's a contagion. Here's a buffoon who got what's coming to him. Here's a man who will remind me of my own addictions. Here's a reason to get healthy so I don't end up *like that guy*.

You know what I saw?

Jesus.

Lemme tell you how:

I was in the middle of one of these trips home to see family where Tara and I invariably cram in too much with too many people. We found out Don was back in the hospital and found out how so many had responded to him. It tends to disgust me, honestly, when people treat folks poorly that they consider beneath their dignity. I have a lot harder time hanging out with the bourgeois than the up and outers and down and outers. It's the suburbs, not the city nor country, that boil my blood. Because this happens. Don dying on a bed in ICU and folks cutting him out of their life.

I'm no hero, just a dude, but I saw Jesus in Don. It wasn't complicated. I went up to his bed, told him who I was in case he'd forgotten, started showing pictures of Tara and our visits with family and friends. I told him why we had come home and the rest. He mouthed his responses to me: trache tube kept him from speaking aloud.

I said, "Don? Can I read some scripture to you and pray over you?"

He nodded.

I read him the words from the daily office, most talk about deliverance from affliction. He asked for prayer and I prayed boldly for his healing (I only started doing this recently after watching a healer point at guys with permanently broken knees and say *Be healed right now in Jesus' name* only to see their knee pop back into place). He asked, mouthing, for a regular chaplain. I got onto the staff and they agreed to regular chaplain visits. He said it was hard seeing no one while in there. I put my hand on his arm and forehead and prayed again.

After all of this, when I locked eyes with him I saw into his soul. There was a young boy in there stuck deep under the dragon scales, his eyes watered and then burned with an intensity so that I felt his very retinas reel me in. Deep calls out to deep. I experienced it there again and wondered what desperation had driven a man so likely to look elsewhere to turn around and lock eyes with one such as me. What he received from the scriptures about affliction and sorrow and God being with him through it all.

Unsure how long we held that gaze, but it was clear: Rabbi, you have the words of life?

To whom else could we go?

A few weeks later they let him talk for the first time. He welcomed his wife and said he'd been depressed, but now *he was healing.*

What will he do with the time that remains, he whom they said deserved to be sick?

What would you do if that were you?

Let's talk a little more about these diabetics who *deserve* to be sick:

Right now, as you read this, a black market thrives. They don't trade guns or bombs or sex slaves or heroin. They trade one another test strips for insulin, sensors for infusion sets, diabetic to diabetic. They do it because of the life-or-death risks: this disease could cause any one of them to go blind, to go into a coma and never wake up, to lose an arm or a kidney. Some say that diabetics deserve it: they're "spoiled brats who continue to ask for bigger and better Mac products as if diabetes is fashion" or whatever the current critique is. Perhaps. Perhaps they deserve it. Perhaps they are the least of the sick. But! As an equal and opposite reaction, the diabetic black market curbs the complications of that bloated and profitable pharmaceutical industry that has rendered it nearly impossible for diabetics like my bride to get the care they need to stay alive. I say this as the man who writes, "**<u>To Keep My Bride Alive</u>**" on the memo line of every check I write them, my own little way of asking *have you no decency, sir?* The diabetes black market often gives some diabetics the only relief they can find from those who profit off of the sick, relief from what Scripture calls "usury" — excessive interest added to an asset for the sake of gouging the poor, the weak, the downtrodden.

Those in need of healing

Because of the existence of this absurdity and others, a street artist with type one diabetes named Appleton has taken to exposing corruption in the system. My bride has type one diabetes— her immune system attacked her beta cells when she was fifteen and she lost the capacity to process sugar. People seldom realize that she didn't get diabetes because of an unhealthy lifestyle. She has type one diabetes for the same reason people with Multiple Sclerosis or lupus have their diseases: it's autoimmune.

It attacked *her*.

Tara has followed this diabetic street artist since the summer we moved to New York and I dug and dug until I found a way to meet him. He's a kind and giant soul who has lived a hard and challenging life — almost forty years with type one diabetes.

His gallery show <u>Out of the Cold</u> opened on the Lower East Side, so I decided to interview both he and my wife. We met with Appleton at Hu Kitchen in Union Square and started talking about the disease that unites he and my wife in its bittersweet way:

The Day They Stopped Looking for a Cure

Tara said, "My favorite piece from your <u>show</u> the other night was the 1921 one. I feel like if I owned a piece of your work, I would want it to be more representative of who I know you are."

"No, I appreciate that," he said.

"The 1921 one — if I had that hanging in my house — I would tell *every person* that came over, 'This is the year they stopped looking for a cure. This is when the bandaid happened. And this is why our entire lives are set up for Big Pharma to make money.' I love the composition of that piece. I think there's a beauty about it but there's a heartwrenching hatred."

"I appreciate that," Appleton said. "Lilly. *Lilly–*" he started.

"Eli Lilly?" I asked.

"Yeah, they financed Frederick Banting's team. They discovered insulin in 1921. Do you think for a second — you know Linus Pauling won a Nobel Prize?

The guy cured a disease, cured polio. No one cures diseases anymore. They're like this: Wait a second — diabetes is an epidemic even in the twenties and thirties? And plenty of people don't even know they have it so they live this weird, uncomfortable life and then they die?"

His art calls out corporate researchers for making money off of the sick through selling care rather than a cure. He also calls out those that prop up the system:

"I *challenge* diabetic organizations that do sponsored events with Lilly. Eli Lilly is sponsoring these events like they *want* to stop a $400 billion industry? So that you and I can someday go get a shot? *The diabetic vaccination?*" People all over the world go, 'Well they're doing amazing things.' Yes they are — but that's maintenance – NOT A CURE. A diabetic cure would cause a global economic breakdown. Every peripheral business that comes out of diabetes — from people who just try to make new blood strips, endocrinologists, dietitians, hospitals, supply manufacturers. My guy at the pharmacy who's always been very dear to me, sells me Lantus without a prescription, sells me sticks and everything, giving them to me at the cheapest price he could get them, just turned me onto these new sticks that are $14 a bottle and this little machine that's like $14. I've got like seven of them at the house because I get tired of looking for them. Even the cheapo meter guys are in on it. It defies logic for the people who gloss over it."

In 2013, $400 million was donated to a diabetic organization. Of that money, only 7% went to cure-related research. The rest?

"Goes to b.s. fundraisers," Appleton said. "Fake 5ks. This one young lady wrote to me, she's a twenty-six-year-old single mom whose daughter is type-one, she said, 'I understand, but it's just the camaraderie.' That I never had and never sought out. I said, 'I get it.' If that's what you're getting out of it — this positive energy — how beautiful is that? But don't be confused."

It reminds me of the "camaraderie" sold *as* Davita dialysis: the stats are with kidney *transplants,* not dialysis. But Davita pretends as if they're creating community by selling days of time in the chair next to other people doing the exact same thing.

Three years ago, Appleton asked an endocrinologist in Los Angeles, 'What are you gonna do when there's a cure?'

The doctor was washing his hands and asked, 'What'd you say?' He wasn't listening.

"He was worried about his golf game later because people will always be diabetic. I asked, 'What are you going to do when there is a cure?'"

He goes, 'What do you mean?'

Appleton said, 'You're an endocrinologist — it's your specialty, right? What are you gonna do if some company in Korea that's been working on it outside the realm of America's Big Pharma, what are you going to do when *they* cure it?' It perplexed this doctor that somebody had that question for him in the first place.

Dumbfounded. I said, 'Isn't there something wrong with that? That you're not bothered by it?' I never saw the guy again after that. He wasn't even like, 'Wouldn't that be great!'"

We all laughed.

"But know there are many, many beautiful doctors and diabetic professionals who truly, truly care and do wonders for all of us diabetics," Appleton said. "Let that be known."

Tara said, "Yes. But of all people that doctor should want a cure."

As Appleton understands it, donations for a cure have dropped off in the last few years because diabetes is being portrayed as easy and not as difficult as it can be, as a nightmare – where every minute of the day you cannot stop being diabetic. In his mind, the lung cancer ads go right to the point – showing lung cancer victims with holes in their throats. People need to be scared that diabetes is a life long challenging nightmare.

"You can live a nice life — but it is a daily battle— mentally and physically – a daily battle. You want people to know more about type one diabetes. That it's not their choice. Sadly smoking that leads to some lung cancers is a often a choice. A woman I met the other day was looking at her daughter's blood sugar in California on her phone."

"Through Dexcom," Tara said.

"You're kidding me! 'Hey honey, are you okay?' Texts her right back. If my mom had that, are you joking me? What are these people gonna do? What's Dexcom gonna do? What's Medtronic gonna do? Are they all dying to go out of business? No. There's a conscious lobby. How powerful is the NRA? How powerful is the Sugar Lobby? The Sugar Lobby gave The World Health Organization — hypocrites — $400 million to change what they considered to be the healthy dose of sugar. They doubled it. That's out there through Freedom of Information Act. Look it up. Ten years ago, five years ago, whenever they put out the stat that said *One gram of sugar a day is okay*. As opposed to whatever's crammed into a Coca Cola. And the Sugar Lobby withheld their money to blackmail World Health into saying *Did we say it was a gram? Why don't we make it two grams?*"

He pantomimed dumping it over an invisible plate.

"Look at all the money. They can't wait for Africa to become diabetic. They can't wait for the Latin American markets. They just can't wait for the Chinese. They have the patent on insulin. A friend of mine just gave me an empty bottle that had Japanese writing on it. I've been dying to get bottles from every country. They're all in English because, guess what? We make the insulin. There's no *generic* insulin."

Appleton used to buy insulin from Canada to get cheaper Lantus. Suddenly, they stopped selling it though they had previously sold it without a prescription.

"That's how they've controlled the world. My endocrinologist knows. He's diabetic. He says, 'All I can do is help *us*. That's what I want to do.' He's a very sought-after guy, speaks a lot, I thoroughly enjoyed him last time we were together. Everyone loves to say to us, 'How is the whole world in on something?' Marketing teams at pharmaceutical companies come up with *restless leg syndrome*. I've shaken my leg since I was five years old. But *now it's something* that a marketing company creates to stop you from shaking your legs. What are you talking about? Who cares that you're shaking your leg? They're not doctors. They're Mad Men."

He pointed to Steven Pressfield's testimony in <u>The War of Art</u>:

Do you regularly ingest any substance, controlled or otherwise, whose aim is the alleviation of depression, anxiety, etc.? I offer the following experience:

I once worked as a writer for a big New York ad agency. Our boss used to tell us: Invent a disease. Come up with the disease, he said, and we can sell the cure.

Attention Deficit Disorder, Seasonal Affective Disorder, Social Anxiety Disorder. These are not diseases, they're marketing ploys. Doctors didn't discover them, copywriters did. Marketing departments did. Drug companies did.

Even for those few looking for a cure, one of the great failings of the American science lab is the lack of shared research. Other countries do it, why don't we? The few people looking for a cure won't share information *because there's still going to be money for a cure.*

"Stem cell research — all of that — is still about corporations making money," Tara said. Tara has people often sharing stuff with her about a cure. "People think about me when they hear diabetes-related stuff, text me, but I don't read anything people send about cures, really."

"You just give up on it?" I asked.

"It's a way of protecting myself from the thought of a cure. I distance myself from the information because I can't think about it in my lifetime. But I distance myself from the article because I can't handle it today. Certain things, if they're shared by other diabetics or in discussion boards about CGMs and stuff, I'll pursue more information along those lines. It's like that guy last night who said, 'I don't read a book about diabetes unless it's recommended to me by a diabetic.' I feel the same way about someone who reads something random and sends it to me — they don't necessarily have diabetes. But if some diabetic has read something, that's a safer gateway. Even if other diabetics post about cure stuff, I don't read any of it. I only read articles that talk about care. Even then I don't read articles about care if it's too much of an emotional investment for me at that point in time."

I'm a writer, a reader, an editor, and a producer, professionally. People send me reading recommendations… often. I got a text from a guy the other day recommending an article. Life is short. Books are many. Why waste time on bad ones? Or bad articles written by still-developing authors yet to be tested by time? So I asked him, "What's this about?"

He said, "I don't know. Sometimes I just see a title of something and send it to someone it reminds me of."

I laughed. I count on the recommendations of friends for *quality* modern pieces and he hadn't even read it. It wasn't a big deal, but in Tara's case, I cannot imagine that frustration tethered to my daily life and health and sanity.

Tara texted mom. "She asked 'How was the diabetic art show?' and I wrote 'it was so beautiful and good.' Lance and I had a horrible fight all afternoon and evening before we got there. I was just a mess. But it wasn't until we walked in the door that I realized I was emotionally and spiritually gearing up for seeing *this*." She pointed to all of the type one artwork.

"Oh wow," Appleton said.

"I didn't realize that I was…"

"And you hadn't seen the earlier show," Appleton said, "which had a lot of the work."

"Right."

"I really like that," he said. Referring to how visceral her reaction was, of course, not that it caused strain in our marriage. Which is really just the strain of diabetes on both of us as people.

"I really had to apologize to him," she said. "My emotions were off the charts because I'm going to this thing that was like *diabetes everywhere* and I didn't connect those two things until I walked in the gallery. But then I texted my mom a picture of all the people that I met. She texted back *all those people have diabetes?* I wanted to start crying reading that. *Yes, type one.* And she was like *That's so cool!* I was thinking *that's HORRIBLE.*"

He laughed. "Right."

"But she meant in terms of the community."

"Of course."

"That's the sweet part is that you're helping foster community. The bitter part is just diabetes."

Appleton said, "When I met that whole little circle of students and young adults, my friend Dan was like, 'Well they're all type one diabetic.' And I said, 'For starters, I'm so sorry to hear that. Thank you for coming down.'"

Appleton keeps creating a third space for that to happen. Tara doesn't know if that was his original intention or not, but Appleton certainly sees himself as an educator and an advocate. Sometimes educating means you have to let others advocate *for you.*

"In high school," Tara said, "I was diagnosed and my friends from youth group and stuff knew I had some issues with the nurse in the hospital, they gave me the wrong-sized needle, I gave an injection that went straight into the muscle and hurt. I stopped giving injections for a month. My parents had to do it. Anyway, my friends knew I had to go on this weekend trip or choir tour or camp or CIY or all of these things that were a part of my life growing up — they had this cooler we could plug into the dashboard of the car that could be hot or cold. The boys would carry my cooler of insulin to the front of the church van or the dorm. My friends from youth group experienced life with me," she said.

"Change," I said.

"Yeah," Tara said. "Me learning and communicating about it because I was processing it. Then they also were the ones who were kind of my buoys or life preservers. They helped me when I was by myself. When you live at a week of camp, when you live at a week of CIY, it's a completely different experience than just seeing me for a few hours a day every few weeks."

"Which is what you mean when you say *they know me*," I suggested.

"Right. In 2009 after a group trip to Thailand, my future boss, Chris DeWelt, said, 'I knew it would be good to be on this trip together so we could get to know each other and coordinate working together in the fall.' Chris and I got to talk about the plan for the department on our flights and stuff, but he was like, 'It wasn't until then that I really could see the ins and outs in how diabetes affected you.' He said it again when Abby [Chris' daughter] became a type one diabetic after her surgery."

That's the fight: seeming normal until she isn't anymore. I remember telling one of her colleagues at the college she had type one diabetes and he said, "I had no idea." There's this diabetic blogger Tara enjoys named Kerri who says, "Of course I'm a normal person, except for the times when I'm not." Meaning that she would like to live a normal life and not be seen as weird, but when a high hits or a low hammers her, it suddenly sends her into this alternative state of being in an *Invasion of the Body Snatchers* kind of way.

Appleton rejected the metaphor because he never feels normal:

"A recent friend I broke up with — she's very important to me — had mentioned the reason was the lack of presence in our relationship. I said, 'What if I said I was dragging around my grandfather and I had to take care of him constantly? My attention would be on this person. But it's on my schizophrenic body.'"

In Greco-Roman times, some murderers would get punished by having the corpse of the victim strapped to them that in walking around tethered, they might rot together. Appleton's pieces mirror that: his body *and the body he must carry*.

"Did I test?" he asked. "What was I an hour ago? I have to memorize my numbers all day. You take a shot at six-o-clock in the morning and you go to bed and you wake up like forty-five-minutes later and you're like, 'Wait a second...' I used to want to get a tattoo that had two boxes and I would just mark an X with a permanent marker for whether or not I gave my shot. And at the end of the day I'd wash it off and make another one the next day. I've been thinking about diabetic tattoos my whole life."

"I heard about tattoos," Tara said. "Since we have an autoimmune disease, some tattoos can be really detrimental because your body is constantly fighting to get rid of the ink. We already have something that attacked part of our body so there's a lot of people with tattoos *and* autoimmune diseases that have a lot of very serious health complications."

"That's good to know," he said. "Thank you for that. I'd never heard that. Trying to heal some wound."

"And your body is already attentive to that sort of thing."

"Yeah. It wasn't before I was diagnosed. Where were you when I needed you?"

She laughed, probably at the image of Appleton getting a tattoo at age nine. Neither of them have tattoos. Both of them expressed interest — even a slight mourning over the fact that they could never get one, never have a legitimate right of refusal. Little details stack up like that and make them both emotional.

Tara said, "I think Lance's assistance and support is invaluable in the day-to-day life. But I do think there's something when I meet a group of diabetics like on [the opening night of Appleton's show]. This makes us instant friends. It's so weird because how many categories of life do that? You could say, *We have the same music tastes*. But it's not that deep. I was talking to a guy the other night who said he would not get an endo who doesn't have type one, but in my experience, I feel like my endo is the only person that isn't a diabetic who actually knows everything it takes for me to stay alive. And that's why I trust them. Not everyone else understands the complications."

Appleton nodded.

"It's a big emotional withdrawal," Tara said. "To access supplies knocks me back. I feel blown over any time I think about attaining supplies or prescriptions or... part of it is just because I'm dealing with this twenty-four-seven and I can't even... I don't even have the energy–"

"To do that," Appleton said.

"To pursue more than how I <u>feel</u>," Tara said, "much less fight companies to get what I need to hopefully feel okay. **It's insult to injury.** I wish there was one person in the supply industry that knew what they were talking about — dosages, nutrition, and supplies — where you could just actually get what you needed and you didn't have to recall and check supplies. We couldn't do what we do without the endocrine team. And I feel incredibly supported by them and they bend over backwards to fill prescriptions and help me with emergency insulin when the pharmacy's hassling me, 'Here's three bottles of promo insulin.' Dr. Hamlett's office has been amazing."

She continued, "But *they* can't control the pharmacy in Target at Atlantic Avenue Barclay's Center illegally changing my prescription. They can do a preauthorization letter for Bayer Contour Next strips to my insurance company, but then Oscar — my insurance company — gets that and decides to leave me an automated voicemail? Saying they've rejected *my preauthorization?* I realize the healthcare industry is always changing things. I realize the insurance is always changing and the pharmacists have to be on top of it too and their computer systems probably can't even keep up with the way that things are changing. Sometimes when I talk to someone in my insurance company, I say, 'I know that this is changing so much, but it is YOUR JOB to know how it's changing. Someone in your office *should know.*' No one in the pharmacy knows who to send a preauth form to or if I have a dosage they can't fill. And then I get a letter in the mail from them that says it's not a medical necessity for me to have these specific test strips when those are the only test strips that communicate with my pump and my CGM and my glucometer? Then I got a letter dated the next day that said they *were* going to approve it. But I get both of them the same day and wonder if I'm going to spend two more hours on the phone with this company to see which one they actually meant. Or should I call the pharmacy to see if they'll fill it? Or is the script from the doctor still rejected? Or should I call the doctor first? The pharmacy first? It's constant."

Diabetics like Appleton and Tara can't run health insurance companies for them too.

The biggest problem with advocating for every part and parcel of the supply chain is that stress raises blood sugar. The actual process of obtaining insulin makes it harder for Tara to process insulin. The belabored process is literally poor care. When Appleton's concerned about his high sugar, that's stress which raises the sugar. You can't give insulin for stress. You have to *try*, but there's no formula for how cortisone affects sugars like there is for carb counting. Stress hormones make your body resistant to insulin. So you're perpetuating that high. Tara knows this as well. It's a sick cycle.

"Having a pharmacist that's on your side and in your corner that is as close to you as a doctor would be is the best," Tara said. "Even if you don't have a doctor who's a great support, you can still get what you need. But if you don't have a pharmacist that's a great support, you can't even get what you need." A doctor's office staff can help. Without someone in your corner at a pharmacy — not even just selling over the counter — but who will just keep making the phone calls to hound the insurance companies you need to access the supplies you need.

Luckily, I'm related to some *great pharmacists* who have helped me over the years — particularly in this recent season when I almost died and have fought medical supply companies for the better part of ten months. But should I have to find a back door through the system in order to get what I need? Shouldn't someone in the medical supply or insurance industry here in New York City be able to do their job? Whatever happened to morally excellent work? There's work ethic and then there's *the ethics of work*. We often just mean "work hard" with work ethic, but if you're working hard to build a machine that kills people — say, a bomb — your work ethic stinks no matter how hard you work. It takes both (1) working hard, (2) at something noble. Or just helpful on a basic day-to-day people with common folk.

Appleton brought in his German Shepherd from outside. Tara said, "We were talking about medical alerts. Almost every diabetic I met at your gallery wasn't wearing stuff. They weren't wearing medical alerts. They weren't wearing their pumps outside. It was only Eric that was visible. As soon as I got there, I was looking for little bruises on people's arms or bumps from the Dexcom or pumps."

"That's funny," Appleton said.

"So when you said, 'The diabetics are here in force tonight,' I decided to be a little more outgoing and introduce myself to someone rather than just looking to see if I could tell. But yeah, only one guy really… pump on the belt loop."

"Nowadays I'm like this." He grabbed his needle and faked like he was going to inject himself with his shirt raised in the middle of Hu Kitchen. "I don't care who you are or where you are. I don't know if you were part of this thing that was on Beyond Type One's site? What I'm about to tell you sounds like it would happen in some less-understanding part of the world, including less evolved parts of New York City. This restaurant posted signs that read, 'Do not take your shots in front of people.' My response to that is if you have to write a note asking diabetics not to take their shots in front of other people, *then most of your clientele is diabetic*. Fact check it. One in four people in the year 2030 will be diabetic. Think about that next time you're in an elevator."

Tara tested: 134. She showed him her pump. In a strange moment of grace, her sugar had been hovering around 134 for the last twelve hours, slowly declining towards 100. It's this beautiful straight descending curve towards normal that we never see, the unicorn of diabetic days — this on the day we were meeting to talk about the disease.

"You gotta figure out the one-thirty-four secret there, Tara," Appleton said. "So awesome."

"I slept the whole night without my pump alarming. I slept *eight hours*," she said.

"I'm glad you said that," he said. "The reason I'm so intrigued is because I thought you had to have the pump then this other beeper. I thought you had to have two units. I gotta do that or it's gonna be the death of me."

A dark shadow passed over both of their eyes like some flashlight had pointed up at both of their faces from below, exposing creepy crawly things hiding under their stone-cold expressions.

Tara said, "When people say, 'You have such great technology!' I always feel a little bit of responsibility in an advocacy standpoint to say, 'Yes, this is amazing and I'm thankful for it, but every day I'm changing a needle or a battery or a sensor or get a prescription refilled from my doctor. There's ten things on me right now.'"

"You can sleep with the pump too?" he asked.

"Mhm," she said.

"Never bothered you at all?"

"No. Two nights ago I got a no delivery, which I rarely get, but that just means the insulin's not getting into me. It's like backed up into the thing."

"Right. I toss and turn so much." Rolling over at night and worrying about tubing shows how all-consuming this disease is.

"It's constantly on your mind," Appleton said. "You're never not diabetic for a minute. You're gonna go somewhere? You gotta test before you go into that meeting. A job interview. When you wake up and when you go to bed. It makes you think about your eyes and your feet and everything else. It's depressing. And it's heavy. And you wish someone was just going, 'Hey man. I'm here. And I know it. And you're here.' In any friendship, it's important that somebody just knows. I hate to be so… *It's a mother #μ¢&ing nightmare*, but it is. A nightmare. And it doesn't have to be if people in your life… I'm always fascinated by… like the kids we met the other night —"

"Exuberant they are," I said.

"Right. And everything's cool. With their maintenance, they may never have the complications…. But I think about people. It's a rich man's disease. You can't be a poor diabetic! You're just gonna eat horrible food. You're probably drinking a dollar soda instead of five-dollar fresh-squeezed orange.

"To get your sugar up?" Tara asked.

"Yeah. Or you might *never* have juice. You might have dollar-ninety-nine for two liters at Costco. Why? Because."

"I must say, you guys are awesome because… to have a partner in this is really… to have somebody who's completely with the program. It's choking me up a little bit actually. It's important that you feel that trust and it doesn't happen that often. **The most important thing about being diabetic is that it can be very lonely.** But it's very hard to just go, *You have no #μ¢&ing idea. You have no idea. You're with me. You take care of me. You ask me how I'm doing — when I'm checking, you're thinking of checking, but that weight…* And you grow up

80

very private too when you're diabetic. So it's not a habit to tell people. It's really not. You're like, *Oh I'm cool. I'll still get high with my friends in high school. Still smoke pot and still drink beer.* You're not going to tell them, *Oh I feel like dog water right now.* You'll just say, *Oh I'm hammered* or *I'm tired.* You wouldn't say anything about diabetes. That's the real weight of it: not feeling that people really know and then feeling so vulnerable that somebody doesn't want to be a part of that life. I'm always cryptic using the word 'friends.'"

"Relationships," Tara said.

"They may see that it's... I've been with friends where it's like, *I can't see right now. Let's just get something to eat, I can barely see.* And I thought it was funny that someone cares for you and knows that. But they may not... they may be selfish and going, 'Do I want to go thirty, forty years with this person? Ten years with this person? Have to take the time out of our lives to maintain something?' And then *oh yeah* you've got to make a living. And then you want to pursue your art. Get in touch with people. Some days it makes me want to just turn off my diabetes for two hours right now to watch a movie?"

"All of this technology is so great," Tara said, "but I'm sick of it. Yeah, I'm thankful it wakes me up when my sugar's dropping or rising and I can fix it faster. But any time someone's like, 'Wow. Aren't you so thankful you're in this technology age?' I'm always like, 'Yes, but this isn't going to go away.' I have to carry a HUGE purse around so I have supplies to replace *every single thing* that I wear on me and then if it breaks — like my pump stopped working Saturday night — it was like, 'Thank goodness I have this stuff.' I plant insulin all over places in New York City so that I can grab it. I'm carrying it with me right now, which I don't know that I should be because of the heat. But…"

It's like she's carrying around a bug-out bag everywhere, but she's not a survivalist. And if she were a survivalist — a prepper — her bug out bag would be twice as huge. I can hear you now: what all could she need, really, Lance?

"Extra pump infusion sets. Reservoirs. An extra lancet to poke my finger in case mine breaks. Syringes and insulin in case my pump breaks. But I only carry short-acting insulin, which is what my pump uses, so if my pump does break, like it did Saturday, I don't have long-acting insulin with me because I'm not going to carry long-acting insulin with me every day. If my glucometer breaks, I can't carry <u>two</u> with me every single day. Sugar. Protein. Extra test strips because sometimes I run out. I unload my purse when I get home and before I leave, take out trash and any extra weight, then refill all of my stuff."

Someone came to visit her here in the city. We were walking a lot, as New Yorkers do — six to ten miles any random day. When we have guests and trekking all over the city, it's easily ten miles. This guest — someone close to her — asked, "Do you ever just leave the house with only your metrocard and I.D. and just not want to schlep stuff all over the place?"

And she said, "I can't because I have diabetes."

And this guest — this person who meant the world to her — started crying.

Tara didn't mean to shame her.

It's just for a moment, that person — a person *who knows about as well as I, her husband, can know* — forgot. Tara doesn't get that luxury. Burrowed into her subconscious is this deep urge to snap awake if her sugar's dropping, all the time, always. That's the burden.

When her pump broke two Saturdays ago, she planned to leave her continuous glucose monitor site in because she didn't want another inch-long needle in her. Once her new pump arrived (it was thankfully under warranty) she planned to reset it, recalibrate it. But then she realized:

"Wait a minute. I could have a little more than twenty-four-hours of *no adhesive on my body at all. No cording. Nothing.*"

So she went for it, tore off the CGM.

"It was such a strange experience for me because it's been so long since a pump went out on me and not since I've gotten the CGM. I was completely untethered and *scared to death* to give Lantus. There's something really freeing about going without a pump and it helped me consider what a cure would be like and it helped me also understand people who don't want to be attached to a pump."

Like Appleton.

Tara feels that anything about diabetes is bittersweet. That's what she told Appleton the first time we met. It's bitter that we're at a [diabetes art show](). It's sweet that his show created community. It's bitter that she has to track down all of these prescriptions and batteries and needles and supplies. But it's sweet that she has tighter control. Her pump breaking was horrible and terrifying, but it was amazing to live a life unconnected to cords, to roll over and roll over all night long while she was sleeping and never worry that night about tearing out an infusion site or to walk by people on the street the next morning without worrying if they're going to tear out her CGM accidentally.

"Nothing about it isn't <u>both</u> bitter and sweet," Tara said.

Kind of like the bitterness, sour stomach, and bad breath that follow the highs that Eli Lilly perpetuates.

Sweet ice cream treats a low.

Appleton gave her the 1921 painting after the show. It hangs in our gallery. We're still praying for a cure.

In the book *The Name of the Wind*, there's a story about a man born blind who got healed of blindness, but because he never associated the things he saw with the roundness, sharpness, or squareness of objects, he *still had to touch them*. In the John 9 text, there's such an emphasis on sound and touch. It reminds me of William Fitzsimmons, the man raised by two very blind, very musical polyinstrumentalists. You often see him close his eyes and furrow his brow on a particularly difficult finger picking lick during a concert. We often learn in scripture of those who hear without understanding, touch without experiencing. Before we get to the John 9 text, I want to deal with the biblical concepts of men, birth, and blindness.

Men, in scripture, are not merely defined by their family role. Not merely as property owners. The problem with the curse of Adam takes a man into the field. He's mingling with the marketplace, obsessed with rising up the social ladders in the public square, his perceived — demonic and chimplike — obsession with the hierarchy. Men, more even then women, get harshly encouraged to diligence and excellence in their occupations, regardless of the occupation. It's Ephesians 6:5-10 that says, "Slaves obey your masters. . .doing the will of God. . .serve wholeheartedly." It's the elders sitting at the gate in Ruth 4:1 "Boaz went up to the town gate and sat there." You know the guys. Hang out in the early morning at Braum's in Carthage or in the battery wall at Sunset Park. It's Proverbs 31:23 "Her husband is respected at the city gate, where he takes his seat" let me repeat "where he takes his seat among the elders of the land." In scripture, grown men as sons have a high bar set for them: Proverbs 10:1 "A wise son brings joy to his father, a foolish son grief to mother." Males are the subject of the census which evaluates military strength – "HERE YE HERE YE! All able-bodied men report in for active duty." Male sons perpetuated life by extending the lineage (think: *Father* Abraham or the *Nation* of Egypt, Moab, Canaan). They believed this to be so important that they broke even crazy bounds of polygamy in order to sire nations. Remember Israel and the four women he kept company with? A Lebanese man once told me that the Chinese symbol for trouble is two women under one roof. . . I've found no evidence in any dialect to suggest that's true, but if it was, you could get a witness from Jacob. Or just from that old MTV show *The Real World*. Or Jersey House Wives. So there's a HUGE expectation on men — especially male sons — to perform to the nth degree. So you know about men.

There wasn't much to know, whatever you think of those biases and assumptions, but let's talk about birth:

In scripture, you find supernatural events like opening closed wombs or overcoming threats surround births such as the purging of the firstborn *multiple times*. Births interpret God's relationship with his people — the God who fathered you, oh City of God, out of Egypt I called my son. The Apostle John appeals to birth imagery multiple times: "Children born not of natural descent or a husbands will. . ." "Flesh gives birth to flesh, but spirit gives birth to spirit. . ." "You must be born again. . ." "everyone born of the spirit. . ." The opposite, of course, comes from Isaiah, "you who conceive trouble and give birth to evil." (59:4-5) or in the Psalms, "he who is *pregnant with evil* and gives birth to trouble." That last one definitely calls to mind Mia in Stephen King's *Dark Tower* who bears a demon to full term and sneaks out at night to feast on frogs and worms and roaches in the swamp near the camp in order to "feed the baby." Regardless, there's a supernatural element to birth. Any woman can testify to this, but there are even miracles surrounding births, not to mention the coin flip of salvation or damnation in birthing imagery. The leaping in the womb at the Visitation of Elizabeth, the siring of children in barren wombs, births of prophets and sages and Messianic fore types like the Maccabean boys. *Oh barren womb rejoice…*

We've got men and birth, now for the kicker: blindness. I was actually, in this survey, rather shocked by how many blind people show up in the bible: Sodomites groping about Lot's house, dim-eyed Isaac tricked by Jacob, Samson's eyes gouged out, the troop of Syrian warriors led to Samaria, temporary blindness of Paul, etc. They're the circus of misfortune in the bible, the carnival of suffering. Ophthalmic diseases get blamed on dust, leading to the laws to take care of the blind – for they are weak and helpless. You find punishment for wrongdoing in other nations, never in Israel, that threatens them with getting stricken blind. Spiritual blindness is the inability to recognize truth. Most are so blind, they don't ever realize their ignorance, the stubbornness, their inattentiveness to God – which is why it takes a miracle to heal them, physically and spiritually and mentally. Only God — ONLY GOD, ONLY GOD — in his mercy reverses blindness in Scripture. No one else. Isaiah 29:18 "Therefore once more I, the Lord, will astound these people with wonder upon wonder. . .the eyes of the blind will see." also in 35:5 "His Spirit will gather them together. . .then will the eyes of the blind be opened."

Got it?

1. High expectations on men.
2. Miracles of salvation or cursing with birth.
3. And God alone takes care of the physically blind and spiritually blind.

And now, a story:

As Jesus went along, he saw a man. blind. . . from birth. Lemme say that again. As Jesus went along, he saw a man.

1. From birth.
2. Who was blind.
3. He saw someone with the highest expectations whose supernatural connection at the time of his birth was the removal of the power of sight by the hand of God.

So:

His disciples asked him, "Rabbi, who sinned, this man or his parents, that he was born blind?"

"Neither this man nor his parents sinned," said Jesus, "but this blindness resulted in the potential for the work of God to be displayed in his life. As long as it is day, we must do the work of him who sent me. Night is coming, when no one can work. While I am in the world, I am the light of the world." Night is coming when no productive man can do anything productive. But Jesus is light.

Having said this he made a hawking sound and spat a massive loogie on the ground. We know it was massive because he made some mud with the saliva, and put it on *both* of the man's eyes. "Go," he told him, "wash in the pool of Siloam."

Remember the touch-factor? As a blind man, how do you know if your hands are clean? Either someone tells you, or you feel them to see how greasy, muddy, clumpy, or gritty they are. Jesus put mud on his eyes and told him to go wash. He touched him because, when blind, touch is how you determine the physical shape and feel of the world.

. . .in the pool of Siloam" (this word means Sent) [pause for reflection. let it soak in.] We'll come back to John's interpretive move there.

So the man. Born blind. Went and washed, and came home seeing.

His neighbors and those who had formerly seen him begging — you know that dirty guy down in Penn Station? That dude with the guitar on Bourbon Street? That blind person who passes in the subway, intentionally whacking people's shins with that infernal cane? The annoying transient with the ancient headphones and SONY walkman? That guy.

"Isn't this the same man who used to sit and beg?" Some claimed that he was. Others said, "No, he only looks like him." So they're going back and forth: it's the man, no it's not, he just looks that way. Dude, I'm telling you, *I know that guy*. He used to sit and beg. Nope, but he could do impersonations of that guy in Penn station if he wanted to, eerie look alike.

But the man himself insisted, "I am the man."

"How then were your eyes opened?" they demanded

He replied, "The man they call, ahem, *Jesus*... made some mud...and put it on my eyes... He told me to go to Siloam and wash. So I went, and washed, and'en I could see."

They freak out: man, born, blind. Does not compute. "Where's this man?"

"I dunno," he said.

They brought to the Pharisees the man who had been blind. Now the day on which Jesus had *made the mud... oh yeah, and opened the man's eyes was the Sabbath.* Therefore the Pharisees also asked the man how he had received his sight.

"Whelp," you can almost hear the guy say. "Let me break this down to you doctors of theology and pastors of large congregations really, really slowly. So. Jesus, right? Jesus. Put mud. On my eyes," the man replied, gesturing over his face slowly, "and I washed, right?" Maybe he blinked blatantly to show the crowd his restored eyelid muscles. "And now... *I see.*"

"This man's not God's: he breaks Sabbath."

Apparently getting *healed* of your unproductivity as a man, cured from your birth curse, and opened in your blindness of spirit and body is hard work. Even though it's all passion, not action. Even though you're just passively receiving, not actively doing anything except belief.

But others asked, "How can a sinner who breaks Sabbath like Jesus do such miraculous signs? Cause it's work on the part of a healer: to make an unproductive man rise multiple castes, to make a birth curse go away, *to make a blind man see*. Think of Zaccheus! Dude can't even buy meds to heal someone else's headache!"

So they're divided, bickering. He broke Sabbath. No he didn't, he's no sinner. Oh yes he is: he's *Satanic*. (Notice how this is the second time people are disagreeing over this. Sound like religious people?)

Finally, in the midst of this yes-he-did-no-he-di'n't garbage, they turned again to the blind man, "What have you to say about Jesus? It was your eyes he opened."

"He's a prophet."

Time out.

We've got the man washing, getting healed.

1) He testifies that he's the man: he's not a stunt double or a look alike.
2) He tells his neighbors what happened. Doesn't know about the man — Jesus — who did it.
3) He tells the story *again* to the Pharisees and the neighbor.
4) They ask him his opinion for the *fifth* time, and he gives it willingly, "He's a prophet."

So John says here something I find absolutely hilarious. "The Jews still STILL did not believe that he had been blind and had received his sight. They sent for this man's parents."

Yeah, that'll help: get mom and dad in here. Fun for the whole family.

"Is this. . .*your* son?" they asked. "Is. . .*this* the one you say was born blind? How is it that now he — this random blind guy everyone knows — can see?"

"Well. . ." the parents answered the religious leaders nervously, cautiously, "we know he's our son. . . and we know he was born blind. But how he can see now, or who opened his eyes, we dunno."

Then they blame shift. It's hilarious:

"Ask him. He's of age. He'll speak fer'imself." John tells us they blameshift because they were afraid of the Jews, for anyone who acknowledged that Jesus was the Christ they had threatened to throw out of the synagogue. That's not just no more church services. That's no more food pantry and unemployment benefits. That's no more prom. No more morning business deals ver coffee. A lot hangs on those meetings. That was why the parents said, "Ask him. He's of age."

A *man* born blind, remember?

Once more — *and with vigor!* — they summon the man who had been born blind. "Give glory to God! Tell the truth!" they shout, "We KNOW Jesus is a sinner."

He replied, "Whether Jesus is a sinner or not, I. don't. know. One thing I do know: I was blind, but now I see!"

Then they asked him, "What did he do to you? How did he open your eyes?"

He answered, "I've told ya already and you didn't listen. Why d'ya wanna hear it again? Do YOU wanna become his disciples too?"

Then they hurled insults at him and said, "You're this fellow's disciple! We're disciples of Moses! We KNOW that God spoke to Moses, but as for this fellow, we don't even know where he comes from."

The man answered, "Now that's absolutely remarkable! You don't know where Jesus comes from, yet Jesus opened my eyes. We know that God doesn't listen to sinner. God listens to the godly man who does his will. Nobody has ever heard of opening the eyes of a

MAN. BORN. BLIND.

Opening the eyes of a man. born. blind. *Opening the eyes of a man. born. blind.* If this man Jesus were not from God, he could do nothing."

To this the religious leaders replied, "You were steeped in sin at birth; how dare you lecture us!" And they threw him out. Remember that phrase? His parents were afraid because the Jews had decided that anyone who acknowledged Jesus would be put out of the synagogue? The consequences of that?

And they threw. Him. Out.

Jesus heard that they had thrown. Him. Out. When Jesus found him, he said, "Do you believe in the Son of Man?"

"Who is he, sir?" the man asked, "Tell me so that I may believe in him."

Jesus said, "You have now seen him; in fact, he is the one speaking with you."

Then the man said, "Lord I believe," and worshipped Jesus.

That word means he bowed down to him, like toward a king, like how the Muslims pray toward Mecca, like the Jews bowed before the Ark — the man who could now see bowed down to Jesus and Jesus accepts his worship as God. I'm assuming he's still laying there, I mean he didn't have enough time to get up by the time Jesus starts talking:

Jesus said, "For judgment I have come into the world, so that the blind—" I'm assuming he pointed here to the man kissing towards him while bowing "—will see and those who see—" Remember how the Pharisees are there with Jesus? Standing up? Not bowing? He points to them perhaps "—will become blind."

Some Pharisees who were with him heard him say this and asked, "What? Are we blind too?"

Jesus said, "If you were blind—" he point to the blind man bowing "—you would not be guilty of sin; but now that you claim you can see—" points to the Pharissees standing "—your guilt remains."

Remember how Siloam meant "sent"? Remember how this man born blind came back bowing down, seeing? Remember how he's clean in his posture, the Pharisees guilty in theirs? What won the day? This blind man didn't even know Jesus until the very end, what was his testimony? What was his catch? What did he see that the others didn't?

One thing I do know. I was blind, but now I see!
One thing I do know. I was blind, but now I see!
One thing I do know. I do know…

Oh and that mother of the wolf? Here's a quick follow up story:

She had the goiter for years, even when I first met her. It grew more and more visible the longer we knew her. I first met her with a different wolf on a different plane. Black wolf, large plane. She had the illness then. Some crazy French witch doctor had indoctrinated her into some health cult and insisted on treating *a goiter* with essential oils. Now, since we're on the topic, I should mention here that homeopathic medicine comes from the Greek word meaning "feels like" or "feels the same" and therefore shares the exact same derivation as sympathetic magic which "feels with" or "feels the same." You pair like with like in order to get a desired effect, sometimes greater or lesser. Voodoo or Hudu in other words: sticking pins in dolls in order to hurt a foe, breaking a stick in order to sink a ship. To that end, the entire government of the United Kingdom *and* Australia did comprehensive surveys on the medicine and they performed no better than the placebo. If homeopathic remedies work, they work only when your body responds to your mind or to someone else's prayer. They have no relevance on actual remedies. Perhaps on the most basic level a bit of mint can fix a sour stomach sometimes, a bit of cinnamon can stabilize blood sugar *a little.*

But it sure as shooting can't cure diabetes or fix a goiter.

An abnormally large thyroid.

Hers, at its peak, was the size of a softball. Maybe even a small volleyball. It needed surgically removed. Fast.

We ended up going on our ten year anniversary to Rome, Tara and I. Having saved up for ten years in a cash envelope, I felt pretty ready to take my bride and enjoy our time doing simple stuff together. A block from the Vatican, which had plenty of free stuff, and $6 for the best pasta of my life. All we ended up paying for was the $300 plane tickets and $25/night inn, more or less. Some blackberry jam from La Verna. The wolf mother met us there and her new husband met us there. Her husband's the man named Andrew in *The Exposed* chapter above. She arrived so sick, a simple walk a few blocks to the Vatican winded her. And I sat down with Andrew one-on-one the first night. His father did endocrine surgery. Lectured on it often at major universities. Andrew pulled me, Tara, and another guy aside the first night while the wolf mother slept and said he couldn't get past the wall of homeopathic charcoal and essential oils and whatnot. So his plan, after Rome, was to take her back to Florida — not New York — and wait until the goiter *forced her into unconsciousness* so that he could rush her to the hospital and have it surgically removed for her. As far as I know, that happened before he died of a heart attack on the set of his dream film.

Did she deserve to keep suffering because of her stubbornness and pride? Because someone *else* had brainwashed her into extreme homeopathy?

That question never entered Andrew's mind. In sickness, he had said, and in health. He attended the sick. She's still alive.

> "The Christian vision of reality was nothing less than — to use the words of Nietzsche — a 'transvaluation of all values,' a complete revision of the moral and conceptual categories by which human beings were to understand themselves and one another and their places within the world. It was — again to use Nietzche's words, but without his sneer — a 'slave revolt in morality.' But it was also, as far as the Christians were concerned, a slave revolt 'from above,' if such a thing could be imagined; for it had been accomplished by a savior who had, as Paul said in his Epistle to the Philippians, willingly exchanged the "form of God" for the "form of a slave," and had thereby overthrown the powers than reigned on high."

— David Bentley Hart

Remember that diabetic on death's door at the start of the chapter? He died in the hospital. But not before he accepted Jesus and affirmed the creed. Perhaps visiting the one many no one else wanted to visit made a difference?

THE EXILE AND REFUGEE.

One of the most adapted stories in our culture is *Les Miserables* by Victor Hugo. Originally a novel, folks have adapted it into 11 spin off books, 5 comics and 2 manga, 35 films, 20 TV shows, 10 animations, 11 radio dramas, 2 musicals, 26 plays, 3 concerts, and 5 video games. My favorite *Les Mis* video game adaptation? The scandalously titled *Inspector Javert and the Oath of Blood*.

(I can almost see John Oliver drum his maniacal fingers together at that one.)

As a novelist myself, it baffles me how anyone could write something so profound, so far-reaching. So radically influential over western culture. Hugo wanted to write a story for the people of France, so he wrote *The Hunchback of Notre Dame*. Then he wanted to write a story for his American friends so he wrote *Les Miserables*. And it is: a story of love and grace in a world that deserves neither. A story about a man getting a second chance in the New World.

What's remarkable to me about Les Mis is the story of exile. Valjean's truly exposed: no home, refugee, the rest. You realize what it's actually like to die from exposure?

To freeze to death like Napoleon's troops as they retreated from Russia?

To overheat and sweat yourself dry?

To be taken over by fire, flood, radiation?

This man stole — he owns the evil he did — in order to feed his sister. Went to prison and escapes the prison work camp. Heads into the wild and steals some silver from a priest — this exile, this homeless convict — gets caught in the act by the local police. Folks that will send him right back to prison. They wake the priest. Show the priest what he stole. Priest says, "It was a gift. And he forgot the best part: the two silver candlesticks."

I'm paraphrasing here.

But of the exiles in the area — the refugees, the homeless — Valjean least deserves the gift of freedom, let alone a fresh start. The priest — in the musical version — says "You must used this precious silver, I have saved your soul for God."

Valjean uses this grace — this radically undeserved gift of freedom and a new life. He does good works *from out of it* that linger on after his death. As some lists of the corporeal works of mercy state: ransom the captive. From having been ransomed, he ransomed.

Lots of folks *choose* to sleep rough. And so we joke about hobos. In fact, a book came out not long ago by John Hodgman called *The Areas of My Expertise*. He, of course, meant the title sarcastically. In it, he gave a list of 700 hobo names.

Here's a sampling:

#1: Stewbuilder Dennis
#2: Cholly the Yegg
#3: Holden the Expert Dreamtwister

#4: The Rza
#5: Jack Skunk
#6: Jack Skunk Fils
#7: Lord Dan X. Still-Standing
#8: Marlon Fitz-fancy
#9: Bazino Bazino, The Kid Whose Hair Is On Fire
#10: Whispering-Lies McGruder
#11: Nit Louse
#12: Dan'l Dinsmore Tackadoo

It goes on for nearly forever. Sure it's fun to joke about that because hobos choose that life. But then again, the joking often turns to tormenting. And tormenting carries over when stereotypes blur the line. Chesterton said:

"Travel ought to combine amusement with instruction; but most travelers are so much amused that they refuse to be instructed. I do not blame them for being amused; it is perfectly natural to be amused at a Dutchman for being Dutch. Where they are wrong is that they take their own amusement seriously. They base on it their serious ideas of international instruction. It was said that the Englishman takes his pleasures sadly; and the pleasure of despising foreigners is one which he takes most sadly of all. He comes to scoff and does not remain to pray, but rather to excommunicate. Hence in international relations there is far too little laughing, and far too much sneering. But I believe that there is a better way which largely consists of laughter; a form of friendship between nations which is actually founded on differences. To hint at some such better way is the only excuse of this book."

Said in another way, it's one thing to laugh at a difference. Indeed, to laugh *together* with those different from you. It's another to sneer. Still another to act out on your sneering: racism is the latter two. Unity in diversity is the first. Not simply diversity as a window dressing, like most New Yorkers who like to be *around* diversity, but not united in light of it. Not actually inviting this polycultural, polyglot city *inside their home*. New Yorkers love to sneer at racist southerners, but they're the ones who still have segregated schools.

The same could be said of the exile, you know: that country of men without countries. It's one thing to laugh at a man who chose to sleep rough for the oddity. Certainly folk laughed at St. Francis. He encouraged it. What do you think a tonsure's for? Fashion? To reduce wind resistance for your prayers to get to heaven faster? Nah, it's there because it looks absolutely, positively ridiculous, that's why. He *encouraged* you to laugh at *his* homelessness and silly haircut. It's one thing to laugh at the difference. But it's another thing to sneer at a man experiencing homelessness and assume he *chose* to be homeless. It takes still a further step into the abyss of hatred to move from the assumption that the vast majority *choose* to be homeless and to act out on that assumption through verbal and financial and physical abuse or neglect. A man experiences homelessness almost always not because he's poor, but because he has no one to be a friend, a neighbor. Because of ignorance and abandonment. And, in my experience, that *includes* hobos who choose to do so: isolation tends to follow abuse. *Into the Wild* shows the desperate, nihilistic need for community someone can have if they choose to live alone.

Let's go back to Will for a second. He sleeps most often outside the Jackie Gleason Depot. Many of the guys who work there — like Mike — treat him as a peer who has no neighbors, whose mind and body need healing. Others talk down to him and throw away his bags and tent and shout at him and kick him and even steal his wallet from him. I can't tell you the number of phones perfectly stable and homed people have stolen from him. The number of times we've had to help him get a new license because someone stole an otherwise empty wallet. They seem to have this twisted sense of thinking that believes *Will-moving-down* **is** *me-moving-up*, a downward mobility aimed at everyone else as if upward mobility is some zero sum game with one clearly delineated winner and one clearly delineated loser. *There can only be one rich man here.* Or man with power and agency. Honor. Fame. Pleasure. As if these things *only* exist in a comparative sense, only exist for the sake of pride. But none of them are zero sum game for the same reason family is not. If family's a zero-sum game — if only I can have family and none of my siblings or parents can — then family doesn't exist. Yet many people treat family this way and so destroy family through their ideal of family, destroy community

102

through their idea of community as Bonhoeffer said. Bonhoeffer also said, to the contrary, if you love one another you create family, you create community. Many from the depot help him, give him tents. Others abuse him. After Will hopped on one bus with $4,000 cash in lottery winnings, he fell asleep and woke up to realize the bus driver had stolen it.

"You sure the driver did it, Lance?"

No one else rode the bus that day on that route that carried Will and he wanted it desperately, so where did it go? Some of the depot guys *begged* him not to file a police report. He did. Cops did nothing. Some have stolen bags and phones from him. Others have charged him exorbitant fees buying Will's $300 in EBT for $200 in cash.

But some of them sit in the middle: having "tried" to help him *once*, they try no longer. A group of the drivers got together to get Will a place since Will doesn't want to stay in the shelters two days in order to get affordable housing. That may seem insane until you realize our homeless shelters are glorified prisons. Often for profit just like our prisons. And if the idea of corporations making millions putting human beings in cages and leaving them there for decades *doesn't* bother you, you need serious therapy. Straight up.

But he didn't want to do that. If you're honest, neither would you. So some of the guys at the depot banded together to find him an apartment he could afford. A room. $300/month. They got it all set up for him.

Will said, "No, I can't."

They got pretty frustrated after all that work and started saying Will didn't want to be off the street. He wanted to be ON the street. He *wanted* to continue experiencing homelessness.

But that's not what he said.

He said he couldn't.

"Will not" states volition or desire. I *will not* because I *will to* stay on the street.

"Should not" states morality or consequence. I *should not* because I *ought* stay on the street.

"Can not" states opportunity or possibility. I *cannot* because I *can only* stay on the street.

It's not that Will didn't want to (it's in the name) or thought it wrong to, but had no chance to.

Why?

It took four years to get a straight answer out of him. Four years. Four years of inviting Will to my house and getting rejected. Four years of him finally coming over and learning to tell people about his real self, to offer up his real name and not La Cucaracha Grande (he calls himself that because he says he can survive nuclear holocaust on the street). Four years of feeding him meals, taking him places, trying to get him in shelters and with a social worker and tents and whatever help we could get him.

I'd asked him before, but after all that time, I asked again: "Will? Did the guys at The Depo offer to get you a house?"

"Yeah, yeah. They definitely did. Yeah."

"Was it three hundred a month?"

"Oh yeah yeah yeah yeah yeah."

"And you can't do that every month?" I asked.

"Of course I can!"

"Then why don't you?"

"Cause I can't afford the *deposit, the deposit.* Paycheck to paycheck. I can't afford to save $300 *extra.*"

"Will," I said, "We will ask the neighbors."

We rallied those we invite to our marathon brunches. They gave $550.

He tried multiple times to get me to give that $550 to him for other meaningless things, but I refused. I told him that if he wanted that money, it was *legally* set aside for his housing. Earmarked. He'd have to either go to a nicer shelter upstate and fill out the paperwork or he'd have to find a place himself and do the same.

He shot down literally every option we gave him over the course of several years. We filled out paperwork for public housing in Messina. He shot it down cause they wouldn't let him smoke inside. Will says, "I eat cigarettes. I don't smoke them." It took awhile for me to realize he meant it figuratively because my father used to chew cigars as a young man. So we tried an apartment complex up the road. They had sort of a communal kitchen, communal bathroom situation. He signed the papers, got ready to go. The landlord rented it out from underneath him for just $25 a month more or something ridiculous. We tried calling the housing office, Will wouldn't deal with them. I pushed him to look, and his pushing — and the $550 burning a hole in the account — pushed me.

But no places came. It's almost impossible to find a place in NYC under $1,400 for a 400 square-foot studio. Meanwhile that amount would get a large 1,400 square foot house in Toledo in two years of payments as of right now.

I tried calling other orgs, but failed there too.

Then Will calls me up and says he found a place for $500/month that only needs first month's rent. He knew we had the amount, so he asked if we could make that happen and I told him of course we could.

It took days of coordinating with the landlord, but I wrote the check in his name. Gave it to Will. Who got rained on while on the street. And thus needed another check. Who then tried, illegally, to cash a check made out to Stephen. Or get others to be a forwarding person for it.

Who made plentiful promises of his plan to go upstate and procrastinated for a month because his stimulus check MIGHT come to the bodega address. Who picked a day to move his stuff three hours north to Binghamton.

Who needed all of his stuff moved out of the Uhaul storage unit he'd been paying $120/month to hold what few worldly possessions he owned — a crockpot, a coat, a couple of vinyls. I called up Paul, a documentary film producer and the man behind the massive Alaska Center for the Performing Arts, to see if we could take his Subaru. Tara had just gotten pregnant so she didn't want me going upstate. This was during a COVID lockdown. And a blizzard. Paul was hesitant with the rain and the snow, being seventy-four. But I drove his car and got all of it loaded up the night before Will's bus.

All but a box of ramen and a box of VHS tapes fit, thank God.

I pulled out and it took about three hours to find a parking spot, but I found one ten blocks away. I went home and collapsed on my bed, crashed.

I get an early morning call from Will. When people have told me in the past about what a cushy life Tara and I have in NYC, how we just get to "live it up" all the time and do whatever we want, I think about Will regularly buzzing my front door at 3am seeing if we'd walked the dog for the night. How many people ring your doorbell after midnight? How long does it train them to stop? Early morning call: "Hey Lance?"

"Yeah Will. How's your bus ride going?"

"I missed the bus."

"You what?"

"I missed it. I missed, it, yeah yeah yeah."

"Why?"

"I just did. Look, see, the way I see it Paul could go up there, drop off my stuff and and and the Landlord could get it out of his car, and I could follow him up once my stimulus—"

"Will, you're talking about a seventy-four year old man that you PROMISED to meet up there and unload your own stuff. This is not an option. Get on the bus and meet him tonight."

"I—"

"TONIGHT! YOU'RE GOING!"

"Okay I'll take the one in the morning. But how will I get my stimulus?"

"I'll mail it to you personally. Check in with me before you go." I called Paul and told him to enjoy his evening in the hotel. Will would show up the next day.

In the morning, I called Will. "Are you on the bus?"

"Yes."

"Good. Paul will meet you." I connected them via phone. The pictures I got back were priceless: old crusty Will with his wiry grey hair, scruffy beard, coke bottle glasses giggling as he unloaded his stuff into his first place in… who knows how long?

One of the worst winters that we've ever had hit New York City: winter of COVID 2020. Ice and snow stacked up almost 18 inches at one point. Frankly, in the city, it was kind of nice to have the subway shut down for something other than the virus. Will made it through for four months off the streets. Then one of the cons of one of the drivers at the Jackie Gleason depot came back to bite him. A driver had asked Will to cash in a winning lotto ticket in his own name earlier in 2020 so that it would go on Will's taxes and not the driver's. He gave Will a couple hundred bucks for his trouble and took the winnings. In 2021 just as winter ended, Will discovered that he had to report having made more than he had ever made in his entire life. All of his Social Security, and all of his disability income for his severe autism and accident and all of his medical benefits were canceled.

He could no longer afford rent.

So the landlord kicked him out.

And now he's experiencing homelessness again on the street by the Jackie Gleason depot. When Jesus says love your enemies and love your neighbors, as Chesterton said they're often then same people, this is one of the situations he means. Will needs good neighbors, not bad ones who exploit him.

"Will not" states volition or desire.

"Should not" states morality or consequence.

"Can not" states opportunity or possibility.

Will didn't say he wouldn't get off the street. He didn't say he shouldn't. Not without good neighbors, even if he *deserves* to be on the street. At some point, all sin and all crime is just the execution of ignorance. Boethius calls that the difference between weak medicine and strong medicine: sometimes it takes an entire lifetime to root out the habits of ignorance. I know a pastor who says you do better if you think of everyone as stupid including yourself. I tend to think you do better if you think of everyone as brilliant, teach to the top of both your and their intelligence, and assume they're ignorant: they simply don't know, often because of either habits or intellectual laziness. Most people aren't stupid, they just *don't want to think things through to the end*. That's true even of mentally handicapped folks that can't do calculus but can, if you let them, do hard philosophy. Will's stuck because he's ignorant of what his neighbors know. *You* needed many neighbors to condescend and help *you* off the street and into a home.

Will *can't*.

Not without you and a lot of friends.

I wish I was cut off for the sake of my countrymen, Paul says.

When I went to college as a freshman, I was three years off the conditioning of the Iraq war and September 11th and the Bush years, thinking — over and again — that we should just *nuke 'em up and let 'em glow*, as one of my more… militant professors once said. Some things had shifted in me: the theater and the romantic poets had saved me from suicide, I had gone on service trips to Native American reservations and had a growing awareness that I grew up pretty poor (my first roommate was a mixed race man that grew up as poor as I did and I had far, far more in common with him than any of my rich white pastor kid classmates whose entire family had attended the college, who had large built-in networks).

But for all of that, I still thought the war should keep going on, still felt very *rah rah U.S.A.* At least in theory. Then I saw what institutions and middle managers can do to poor individuals who want a simple summer job to pay off school: refuse to hire him for simply not owning a suit and saying he hoped they would hire him on whether or not he had charm, rather than specific clothing.

So I ended up going to Dearborn, Michigan on support with a young couple to work among refugees of the Lebanese civil war, the first Gulf war, Iraqi refugees from the Iraq war, Yemen from the bombing raids (which I hadn't even *known* about, and they're still going on). It really only takes a couple of conversations to realize you're reading the Bible very, very wrongly. It takes a seven-year-old Iraqi kid, whose mom got wiped out in a firebombing run, kicking your butt in soccer to realize you know nothing about the world. It takes a young Palestinian mother persecuted because she's considering converting to Christianity. It takes teaching an English class and citizenship class thinking you're teaching some poor wretches and realizing, halfway through the summer semester, that one's a surgeon, one's a lawyer, one's an engineer, one's an accountant, one's a professor, one's a poet laureate, one's a millionaire farmer, one's a businessman, one's a computer programmer. All they needed from me was practice pronouncing words. Still another Palestinian Christian evangelist who *worked* with me on the streets told me the Zionists shoot at his house and the Muslims shoot rockets from his house, and both end up destroying Palestinian Christians. But he hadn't lost hope until he woke up one morning greeted by his brothers and sisters in Christ: an Israeli tank rolled up to his front door with a banner reading THIS TANK SUPPORTED BY THE AMERICAN EVANGELICAL CHURCH.

Reread that. Once more. If you can't commit to *at least* not killing your brothers and sisters in Christ, what are you doing? Do you realize how many Christians live in Iran? Iraq? Egypt? And what of the brotherhood of man beyond that? The founder of our alma mater once said to a stranger, "Thank you brother."

A cofounder said, "How do you know he's a Christian?"

And our founder said, "If I didn't hit him in Jesus, I hit him in Adam."

Where has that attitude gone?

Right now, countless people post on social media about how "illegals" are taking away their whatever. Or spreading disease. Or ruining the country. The list goes on. I won't, in this case, condescend to argue those asinine points because at some point, argument glorifies the terms by which the debate is set.

I want to reset the debate:

Jesus.

Was a refugee.

He was. Straight up. He fled to Egypt with his family and died as a homeless, brown-skinned semitic refugee.

What does the Bible say about refugees? You may talk all the time of people breaking the *laws of the land*, but what of the laws of God? And this, frankly, applies to all sorts of refugees macro and micro: if you're worried about your neighborhood "going to the dogs," if you're worried about shifting demographics in your county, if you're worried about the "rough side of town," if you're worried about — as one of my relatives said — the "riff raff" in the first town over from yours, if you're worried about any sort of outsider getting into your inside, if you're worried about people in your neighborhood being "raised wrong" or the way they take care of their yard or house or kids or whatever, these verses apply to you. They apply to the "progressive" New Yorker who cares so much about where their kids go to school that they end up segregating them and they apply to the conservative Evangelical paster I know from Louisville who refuses to send their kids to the school in the "rough side of town." What does the Bible say about the outsider?

I'll give you a hint, it's not a little. My college buddy Eddy G and his wife Emilie who work with refugees compiled this list:

Leviticus 19:33-34

When a foreigner resides among you *in your land*, do not mistreat them. The foreigner residing among you *must be treated as **your** native born*. Love them as yourself for you were foreigners in Egypt. I am the Lord your God.

God directly connects your salvation to this issue: forgive as you've been forgiven. *You* are a refugee from the land of sin and death and darkness. You had better welcome people likewise, otherwise God may not treat you as one native born in Heaven and deport you to the other place.

Isaiah 25:4

You have been a refuge for the poor, a refuge for the needy in their distress, a shelter from the storm and a shade from the heat. For the breath of the ruthless is like a storm driving against a wall and like the heat of the desert.

Psalms 105:12-14

When they were but few in number,
few indeed, and strangers in it,
they wandered from nation to nation,
from one kingdom to another.

He allowed no one to oppress them;
for their sake he rebuked kings:

Genesis 12:1

The call of Abram: "Go from your country and your kindred and your father's house to the land that I will show you."

Exodus 12:49 and Leviticus 24:22

There shall be one law for the native and for the alien who resides among you.

Deuteronomy 10:18-19

For the Lord your God... loves the strangers, providing them food and clothing. You shall also love the stranger, for you were strangers in the land of Egypt.

Jeremiah 7:5-7

If you do not oppress the foreigner... then I will dwell with you in this place...

That's connected to the presence of God in prayer.

Romans 12:13

Mark of the true Christian: "Extend hospitality to strangers." Some versions say "practice hospitality to strangers." It's a commandment in the New Testament. An imperative as essential as love your enemy or thou shalt not murder.

Ephesians 2:12-20

Remember that at that time **you were separate from Christ, excluded from citizenship** in Israel and foreigners to the covenants of the promise, without hope and without God in the world. But now in Christ Jesus you who once were far away have been brought near by the blood of Christ.

For he himself is our peace, who has made the two groups one and has destroyed the barrier, the dividing wall of hostility, by setting aside in his flesh the law with its commands and regulations. His purpose was **to create in himself one new humanity** out of the two, thus making peace, and in one body to reconcile both of them to God through the cross, by which he put to death their hostility. He came and preached peace to you who were far away and peace to those who were near. For through him we both have access to the Father by one Spirit.

Consequently, you are no longer foreigners and strangers, but fellow citizens with God's people and also members of his household, built on the foundation of the apostles and prophets, with Christ Jesus himself as the chief cornerstone.

Exodus 22:21

Do not mistreat or oppress a foreigner, for you were foreigners in Egypt.

Deuteronomy 1:16

And I charged your judges at that time, "Hear the disputes between your people and **judge fairly**, whether the case is between two Israelites or between an Israelite and a foreigner residing among you.

Deuteronomy 10:17-19

For the Lord your God is God of gods and Lord of lords, the great God, mighty and awesome, who shows no partiality and accepts no bribes. He defends the cause of the fatherless and the widow, and **loves the foreigner** residing among you, giving them food and clothing. And you are to love those who are foreigners, for you yourselves were foreigners in Egypt.

Deuteronomy 14:28-29

At the end of every three years, bring all the tithes of that year's produce and store it in your towns, so that the Levites (who have no allotment or inheritance of their own) and the foreigners, the fatherless and the widows who live in your towns may come and eat and be satisfied, and so that the Lord your God may bless you in all the work of your hands.

Exodus 23:12

Six days do your work, but on the seventh day do not work, so that your ox and your donkey may rest, and so that the slave born in your household and **the foreigner living among you may be refreshed.**

Leviticus 19:10

Do not go over your vineyard a second time or pick up the grapes that have fallen. Leave them for the poor and the foreigner. I am the Lord your God.

Literally, that verse applies to all of the hateful things Americans have said about cherry pickers and apple pickers over the years.

Deuteronomy 24:17

Do not deprive the foreigner or the fatherless of justice, or take the cloak of the widow as a pledge.

Deuteronomy 24:19

When you are harvesting in your field and you overlook a sheaf, do not go back to get it. Leave it for the foreigner, the fatherless and the widow, so that the Lord your God may bless you in all the work of your hands.

Ruth 2:9-11

Watch the field where the men are harvesting, and follow along after the women. I have told the men not to lay a hand on you. And whenever you are thirsty, go and get a drink from the water jars the men have filled."

At this, she bowed down with her face to the ground. She asked him, "Why have I found such favor in your eyes that you notice me—a foreigner?"

Boaz replied, "I've been told all about what you have done for your mother-in-law since the death of your husband—how you left your father and mother and your homeland and came to live with a people you did not know before.

Rahab the foreigner was Boaz's mother. Ruth the foreigner was King David's great-grandmother. Both women show up in the lineage of Jesus.

I could go on and on and on. Obviously those verses included bits about those experiencing homelessness and those who are hungry and sick and even in jail. But suffice to say, the Biblical evidence isn't on the side of building walls, excluding school enrollment, refusing entry at airport, eliminating citizenship — or making it hard, cherry picking the foreigners we'd like (such as the ones that will most help *our* economy and *our* society), giving aid over after disproportionate trade agreements (see above in the hunger section, since we're all global citizens at this point), or any number of other gestures aimed *at* and *against* the outsider from liberals and conservatives alike.

Scripture doesn't have time for that.

Kenyan runner Abel Mutai was in first place only a few meters from the finish line, but got confused with the languages of the signs and stopped, thinking he had finished the race. The Spanish runner, Ivan Fernandez, was right behind him. He realized what was going on, started shouting to the Kenyan in Spanish to keep running. Mutai did not know Spanish. He did not understand.

Fernandez, while running, comprehended this *and literally pushed Mutai the rest of the way to victory.*

A report asked Ivan, "Why did you do this?"

Ivan replied, "My dream is that one day we can have some sort of community life where we push ourselves and also others to win."

The reporter insisted, "But why did you let the Kenyan win?"

Ivan replied, "I didn't *let* him win, he was going to win. The race was his."

The reporter insisted, asking again, "But you could have won!"

Ivan looked at him and said, "But what would be the merit of my victory? What would be the honor of this medal? What would my Mother think of it?"

Go out into the street, into the dodgy town, the refugee camp, the dark side of the county, the rough side of Louisville, the school district you fear, cross the border, venture forth. Then bring the foreigner *to your doorstep* and say, "Welcome home." Help him win.

It's the least you can do.

Jesus did it to you.

THE CONVICT.

Let's return to Jean Valjean in Les Miserables. The man of grace in the story is the *ex con*. He is changed and gets new life. The man of law in the story is the cop. He commits suicide. Similar thing with Tale of Two Cities, only the place gets reversed.

It's the man who had a crush on the innocent belle and who does not end up with her, but watches as a French exile from the Napoleonic wars marries her. Who drinks himself half to death and makes a fool out of himself the whole story. Whom the town has come to despise as good for nothing.

This man, when the husband of his high school sweetheart gets exposed as a former French spy, *decides to swap places* with said husband of said high school sweetheart. The fool goes to jail in the prince's place, inverting the fairy tale, taking on the husband's death sentence. And right before the noose drops, the drunken town slob says, "It is a far, far betting thing I do than I have ever done. It is a far, far better rest I go to than I have ever gone."

Dickens inverts it.

It's not just that what we do unto the least of these we do unto Jesus. It's that, having been forgiven, when the least of these act upon the grace they receive they do *as Jesus for us* what Jesus does unto us. Sometimes the ex-convict *saves us*. Our society is built by ex-cons that got another chance, just ask Georgia and Australia. It's built by undeserving hungry who got one more meal, just ask my Irish ancestors who fled the potato famine that falls under definitions *b* through *e* of genocide by the United Nations charter. It's built by those drinking themselves to death who got one more chance at hydration, just ask Robert Downey Jr. And Eminem. To exiles and undocumented migrants again like my Irish ancestors escaping the potato genocide finding a chance in the New World, but also Sicilians when they were hated and the Chinese and Hispanics and even the hometown Alaska Native. To self-inflicting diabetics brought back from the edge in order to give life.

When given half a chance, half a grace, the scoundrel can do for us a far, far better thing than I or you have ever done and in so doing go to a better rest than they have ever known.

Don't believe me?

What bothers us about Javier isn't that he's different than Valjean. What bothers us is that he's the same. What bothers us about Judas isn't that he's different than Peter: they're both shufflers from poor families who asked all-to-practical questions of this God who had a very impractical plan to take on our meat and bones and then die whereupon, manumission fee having been paid for our civic debt, we all might rise with the risen slave. The difference between Javier and Valjean — Judas and Peter — is simply that the latter received the forgiveness offered him and the former refuses it and condemned himself.

Does it hit close to home yet?

What bothers you about the convict isn't the convict getting forgiveness.

What bothers you is knowing, deep down, you're a worse sinner than the worst convict. What bothers the person with PTSD is not the trauma of something experienced passively — that tends to manifest as other trauma such as with abuse victims. What happens to the person with PTSD (and this includes convicts) is growing up in a sweet home and then one day watching *their own hands* commit some atrocity like war. As if their *own body* betrayed them, they stir their ability for incredible evil. The sooner you realize that, the sooner you're free. The sooner you realize that, the sooner you'll see yourself loving those in chains. Paul understood this on multiple fronts. He called himself the worst of sinners, which is accurate for everyone living with a first-person perspective (read: everyone). He also said he carried himself with a sober mind realizing what great evil could come out of him. If the convict — if Peter, the dude who tried to break Jesus out against his will so frequently and fully that he denied his Lord thrice — gets freed, then you do too. Because you too are the betrayer. The leaver. The convict is you. You aren't Peter. You're Judas. I'm Judas. The only difference is if we accept the grace given us. You get forgiven if the convict does because, as Nathan said to David, *you **are** the man.* YOU are as guilty as anyone else.

Isn't it great the Jesus condescended to pay the manumission fee for a convict like you from the maximum security prison house of death?

One spring, I met an attorney whose story calls to mind that old Chesterton and Lewis thinking: What are we progressing towards? Truth, beauty, and goodness?

Or the edge of a cliff?

His name's Bobby Constantino, and as I dig into his life's particulars, I keep learning disturbing lessons about myself and our society.

Six years ago his life and career took off beautifully. After serving in the criminal court's trenches in Boston for ten years, an elite national justice organization in New York City hired him: the Vera Institute of Justice. The New York Times featured his work as a national model, he earned a good salary with benefits, paid off much of his student loans.

Then he quit. Blew the whistle.

Torched all of his professional connections.

Six years later he's still at it, working at restaurants, living paycheck to paycheck, subletting from friends, refusing to go back into the law.

What happened?

Why would a man who had it made turn on his profession, his employers, and colleagues? His decision has already cost him a marriage, an apartment, his credit score, his health insurance — the guy's currently sleeping on couches, living out of a computer bag — and yet he's still adamant he's right.

Why?

Let's sit at his feet together:

St. Anselm College occupies four-hundred acres in the Manchester, New Hampshire countryside. A Benedictine institution home to a monastery and ivy-covered red brick buildings. Its aesthetics call to mind Xavier's School for Gifted Youngsters.

Forty miles south, Bobby grew up in North Andover, Massachusetts. "Well-to-do, leafy, and very suburban," is how he describes it. He was attracted to undergrad studies at St. Anselm College because it was between his hometown and the White Mountains.

"Back then, Boomers like my dad were shouting, 'BUSINESS! ECONOMICS! COMPUTER APPS! PICK SOMETHING USEFUL!' But I took all of those classes and I hated them. There was this required seminar, though, called Great Books, and I loved it. It was Socratic method. The students argued and debated all class long while the monks mediated. Ancient Roman and Greek texts, and other cool stuff."

Father Jerome, sensing Bobby's connection to the material, alerted him to a major in the philosophy department where he could dissect great works on virtue, ontology, citizenship, and such, full time.

"We were reading Aristotle, Cicero, Plato, Bentham, Hobbes, and Mill, and the question we kept returning to was: how do we as citizens lead meaningful lives? What is our place in the polity? How can we live in such a way that we can look back on our lives the day we die and say, 'I'm proud to tell my kids how I lived?

"This will come full circle later, but I, like so many, thought politics was the way. Our whole lives we're inundated with this notion that democracy works. If the people express their will, it will be heard. That's the way to achieve change in a great society."

He interned for a congressman. That office hired him out of college for data entry and occasionally to drive the legislator to the airport.

On one such ride, the congressman told him to go into law school so that he could learn how to write, file, and pass legislation. He got into Suffolk University Law School in Boston — a "home-grown factory for politicians and legal-types across the street from the Statehouse on Beacon Hill."

"Remember, this is around the same time Bill and Hillary Clinton are telling everyone that will listen that 'superpredators' are wreaking havoc in America's urban centers. Sports, T.V., and the movies glorified law enforcement and the military as the best, most honorable ways to protect the public from danger. All these shows on T.V. about gangs — Bad Boys, C.O.P.S., Lockup — and in my earnest, do-gooder head I'm like: I want to help! Where do I sign up?"

The Suffolk County District Attorney's Office covered many of the Boston neighborhoods that were on the news at night in the suburbs: Roxbury, Dorchester, Mattapan— breaking news interruptions that flashed up on the TV with sirens, flashing lights, yellow police tape, and leering mugshots of suspects.

After he graduated and passed the bar exam, the DA's office hired him as a prosecutor.

That's when things got…interesting.

"Day one I'm in court and our philosophy is max bail, max jail. Shootings have been going up for several years, so we need to bring the hammer down on anyone in the vicinity of a gun. The police are conducting aggressive raids and sweeps like you'd see in wartime — busting doors at four in the morning with battering rams, rushing in with assault weapons, throwing everyone down — and we're doing our part in court to take people off the street with mandatory minimums and statutory enhancements."

"Only there's a problem with the narrative undergirding all of this: we're constantly re-upping the pressure with raids and sweeps — Operation Bad Apple, Operation Clean Slate, Operation Rolling Thunder, etc. — but shootings keep getting worse every year. And I'm in the trial session two to three days a week and none of our witnesses are showing up. We're empaneling juries and half of them are looking at us like they hate our guts before we've even given our opening statements. And this is bad, really bad, because making cases at trial is the whole point of the criminal justice system. If our witnesses don't show up, and jurors hate us, we can't meet our burden of proof. And if we can't meet our burden, all of our arrests, exhibits, undercover investigations, and military operations are a complete waste of time and effort.

"So I'm thinking all I have to do is tell everyone — friends, family, colleagues, and the like — what's up. Our aggressive crackdowns and sweeps are undermining the purpose of the public safety apparatus. I mean, I'm right there on the front lines witnessing it every day, so they're obviously going to listen to me…"

He cashed in his state retirement fund and resigned. He hoped to cast light on how aggressive law enforcement tactics alienate communities the system needs to function properly. "So now I'm unemployed, sending unsolicited op-eds to every newspaper editor in the region, screaming at the top of my lungs: 'Everything we're being told, everything we're doing in court, it's all wrong!' And I'm thinking they're all gonna be like, "Oh my God, you're so right!""

But everyone replied something along the lines of are you an idiot? Haven't you seen C.O.P.S.?

Determined to prove them wrong, he moved into the neighborhood where he had worked as a prosecutor, on the Dorchester/Roxbury line.

Bobby moved into an old three-decker on the corner of Quincy Street and Columbia Road — a house former police colleagues told him was "a crack den." He grew close with the guys who lived in the house and surrounding area and raised money to open a program in the courthouse to help them get jobs, G.E.D.s, build resumes, and go on interviews. At the time he suspected that this would help them succeed more than police officers with battering rams cracking down their doors. Bobby wrote up a one-page concept paper and went to see the presiding judge in Roxbury, Eddy Redd.

As a Roxbury native, Judge Redd understood.

When Bobby was a prosecutor, Judge Redd held the bench one day when the police hauled in a guy from Worcester, 50 miles away. They'd issued a warrant because the guy owed money to Roxbury Court many years prior.

"The man goes to court Tuesday after being in jail for a three-day weekend. No job. Not a nickel on him. It's pouring rain.

"Judge Redd waives the money he owes in exchange for time served and then has to pool his own money with the clerk to get the man a bus ticket home."

"Thousands of dollars in police overtime, processing fees, etc., drove him halfway across the state – for what? A few bucks the guy can't pay?"

Living in the neighborhood, Bobby noticed programs designed to reach young men at risk of gun violence weren't offering strong incentives to participate. He also knew, from his days in court, that probation officers threatened to issue warrants if probationers didn't pay their court fees and fines, so he pitched an idea to Judge Redd: offer credit for monies owed to the court in exchange for building resumes, going on job interviews, etc.

It was hugely successful.

"Guys on Boston Police's Most Wanted list start showing up to class every day, building resumes, going on job interviews, and rebuilding their lives."

(He's not bragging: The New York Times featured his program as a national model for states to follow, as did the Brennan Center for Justice in a national practitioner's toolkit).

But at the time Bobby couldn't raise any money to keep the program going, and it baffled him. He thought the true goal of the system was to break the cycle of recidivism and incarceration. He had no clue, in those days, that he was reinventing the wheel, that a program like his, only much bigger, and much more successful, had once ended teen gun violence in Boston for two straight years.

Then he showed up to class one day in 2008, and realized all of his progress with the guys was about to unravel.

"[They're] talking about going out on a mission, getting everybody. I roll up and I'm like, 'Woah, woah. Hold up-'"

The guys had been working with Bobby for several weeks at that point, going to interviews, getting jobs, doing great. The court had waived some of their debt. Now they're talking about going out and getting involved in a beef that's flaring up.

"What happened?" he asked.

In Orchard Park — a housing development by the courthouse — a child uninvolved and unconnected to gangs, Soheil Turner, was standing on the corner waiting for his school bus when a teen from a nearby rival neighborhood walked up and shot him in the back of the head, killing him instantly.

Bobby talked to his men for three hours trying to walk them back. He went home exhausted, furious. In the course of reading articles about the incident online, he came across something that shook him to the core: a report called "Losing Faith."

In 2008, prior to Soheil's killing, a pair of Harvard criminologists wrote a report about a program called Operation Ceasefire, responsible for what had been coined "The Boston Miracle." In the mid-'90s, Boston Police partnered with clergy and service providers, rounded up all of the young people involved in gun violence and presented them a clear-cut choice: jobs and services or nighttime no-knock raids.

It's difficult to fathom what happened next: two years and five months went by in the City of Boston without a single teenager being shot to death.

"Not a single teenager," Bobby said, "not one teenager was killed for twenty-nine months following the first meeting — which is unheard-of in those days, the mid-late 90's, because youth violence was in full-on recrudescence, portrayed in mainstream culture as a war-zone scourge roiling our nation's cities. Yet here was a program that ended it virtually overnight, with rock-solid data backing it, and the BPD axed it."

Could a city like Boston, with its progressive reputation, universities, and culture, really stand by and watch young people die needlessly for two decades?

And yet, here's the Harvard report saying just that:

Our basic conclusion is not that the Boston model of the 1990s has failed, but rather that the City of Boston and the Boston Police failed to pursue the policies and practices that had been so successful during the 1990s.

Gun killings spiked on the graph after it ended.

It gets worse.

CeaseFire also happened in Chicago. You know, the Chicago that gets cited all the time for its gun violence? Chicago solved the problem eighteen years ago with an identical initiative:

Formed in 1999... violence interrupters worked on the street, mediating conflicts between gangs.... Crime mapping found decreases in the size and intensity of shooting hot spots due to the program [up to 73% and decreases of retaliation killings of 100%] in more than half of the sites.

Ever heard of Baltimore? As in The Wire? Same thing happened with a program called Safe Streets (the original link to that study went dead when I posted a test version of this earlier in the week, which leads me to believe the people in power don't want it shared, so I've updated this post to include a link straight to the PDF, which you should copy and share as widely as possible).

McElderry Park did not experience a homicide during the first 22 months of program implementation...However, homicides increased during the period when program supervisors and staff also concerned themselves with a new Safe Streets site in bordering Madison-Eastend where gang violence surged.

(Meaning the program's effectiveness is directly related to whether or not it is sufficiently staffed and funded.) Bobby sent me report after report — the amount of consistent data eclipsed the mind: we know how to solve inner city gun violence.

For instance, the Queensbridge Houses, one of the nation's largest public housing projects, is celebrating what the mayor is calling "A Year of Golden Silence" thanks to a community-based 696 Queensbridge neighborhood peacekeeping program. Added to the data that shows delays in the solving of murders in African-American neighborhoods is race-based, it paints the kind of picture that would make an Old Testament prophet's blood boil. When talking to Bobby, I'm reminded of Jeremiah who called justice and right a fire pent up in my bones: I'm weary of holding it in; indeed I cannot.

Limping along with the program in Boston, unable to figure out why he couldn't raise any money, Bobby caught a break with a seed money grant: $175,000 for three years. It covered half of his program's annual budget. All he needed to do was to use that seed money as leverage to raise the rest.

"We couldn't find a single other funder in the city."

The same problem Baltimore encountered — a brilliant program, spread too thin — hit Bobby. But why? Why were these cities – all with serious gun violence problems – giving short shrift to programs they knew saved lives?

Why were they cutting and underfunding rather than scaling up?

And how did they keep getting away with it?

Then 15-year-old Soheil Turner was killed.

Back in Boson, Bobby's worried his guys are considering revenge. He's texting them and getting no response.

"Meanwhile, I turn on the TV and the mayor's holding a press conference while Soheil's parents are sobbing across town, claiming he doesn't know how something like this could happen in Boston…"

Bobby loses it.

"That innocent child would not have been shot and killed if these programs hadn't been discontinued by the police. These are exactly the kinds of retaliation killings these programs prevent. I know these kinds of killings would not keep happening, because later that night one of my guys texted me, said he'd stayed in with his girl, told me that all the guys decided that afternoon they weren't going to get into it with DSP."

(DSP stands for Dudley Street Park, the rival neighborhood where the suspected killer, who was later arrested and charged with murder, was from.

Bobby wrote a blog post in a blind rage and posted it without thinking about the consequences. A local news outlet picked it up.

"Next thing I know, the link to the Harvard report in my blog goes dead and now I'm persona non grata in the City of Boston. I'm going to these meetings and people are looking at me funny and whispering. The change was palpable."

(Interestingly, as mentioned elsewhere in this post, I posted a temporary version of this article to see how it looked and several links immediately went dead then as well — we've since shored up as many as possible with alternative links.)

Joel asked, "Do you think this is because you linked to the fact that this sort of thing had already happened?"

"It was the way I wrote it," Bobby said. "It's both. You don't embarrass the mayor of the City of Boston if you want to be connected to the funding, the in-circle of academics and think tanks. I named him in the blog post and then the guy who reposted it titled it, 'Dorchester Resident to Menino: J'accuse!'"

I dug around and found the original from 2009. Universal Hub said:

Bobby Constantino cannot believe that Tom Menino keeps saying he knows all the neighborhoods when teens like Soheil Turner keep getting gunned down, he says Menino should resign.

They quoted Bobby's post. You can sense Bobby's rage:

You fell asleep. You gave up on [violence prevention], and the whole thing fell apart. A report out of Harvard is the smoking gun.

You'll notice Bobby's right — that link is, in fact, dead. No worries — I posted the report again on my site. (I highly recommend you download the file and spread it around as far as you can — it's obvious why cities like Boston want such information buried). They since removed his name from a multivariate analysis proving all of this that they have also suppressed. For the record, the community appears privy to this knowledge. The first comment on that Universal Hub post said:

An upper level law enforcement officer told me about 2-3 years ago that Boston had a working system. A combination of politics, turnover, and "I didn't think of it" attitude led them to drop the statistical crime tracking the city was doing and he said — watch out — we're going have a repeat of what happened 10-15 years ago as a result. ...It does sound like a lack of stewardship at some level is leading us back to a very scary future.

Bobby sensed he'd been 86'ed behind the scenes. The program was running on fumes and despite his success with the guys he couldn't raise the remainder. Fearing this would continue as long as the sitting mayor held office (which in Boston usually meant life) he applied for jobs outside Massachusetts. One organization that showed interest in his work was the Vera Institute of Justice, an organization that runs demonstration projects with innovative ideas to test whether or not they work.

Vera made its name in the 70's dismantling New York City's broken bail system, a fact that augured poorly for what little faith Bobby had remaining. "We're now seeing the same broken bail system Vera made its name reforming 40 years ago roaring back into action, incarcerating poor New Yorkers for having no money, its abuses critiqued on all sides by justice writers and reformers." (And getting rid of bail is only the start).

"I'm in New York City pounding the political pavement. I'm meeting with Herb Sturz, one of the founders of Vera. We're meeting with Mayor Bloomberg's criminal justice czar, meeting with probation. All of the big wigs in New York City and they're like, 'This is a great idea, we want do this.'"

Time came to vet it with legal at Vera.

"They look it up and conclude we can't do this program in New York because a criminal procedure law states that no fees, fines, or surcharges can be waived under any circumstances. They get sent to civil judgment here, which means a collections agency's responsible for chasing them down instead of a probation officer, a reform New York considered 'progressive' back in the day."

It reminds me of something comedian John Oliver said recently: "If you want to do something evil, hide it in something boring."

"Six months of work, all these people on board, our stakeholders in New York aren't worried the model will violate the CPL (because the monies are going to be credited by judges in court, not waived), and our own legal department nixes it." Which coincided with Bobby's experience in Louisiana:

"We were contacted by PEW and the Bureau of Justice Assistance to go into different states to do justice reinvestment."

Justice reinvestment finds states with prison beds occupied by nonviolent offenders, releases them safely, and then reinvests that money in programs like Boston's to prevent recidivism.

They come up with this package.

Vet it with everyone.

Over the course of a year, victims' groups, sheriffs, DAs, law enforcement — everyone down in rural Louisiana gets on board.

"I'm going fishing and to LSU games with all of these stakeholders and they're thrilled because Louisiana is the per-capita incarceration capital of the free world and they're embarrassed. They love their state, they're proud of it, they don't want to be known as the 'crown jewel of incarceration'. We vetted this legislative package and we're about to introduce the bills to the house criminal justice committee at the Capitol in Baton Rouge. And then, as we show up in the morning to testify, we learn the D.A.s and sheriffs have gone behind the commission's back and put in red cards, after promising for months to take no position."

It was an act of sabotage that appeared to surprise even the state's Corrections Secretary, Jimmy LeBlanc, who told a reporter the next morning:

"I thought we had a consensus when we went."

But why would the sheriffs and the DA's do that?

"If the commission's reforms passed, the sheriffs would have lost X thousands of inmates, which represented X number of per diems (the state was paying the local sheriffs $24.39 per day for every overflow inmate they housed in local jails). So what probably happened was the sheriffs ran the final numbers, realized how many staff, computers, guns, and military carriers they'd lose if the commission's bills passed, and then went to the governor behind the scenes and said, 'Hey man, you can't support these measures,' and the governor backed down."

Why wouldn't the governor stand up to them?

"Because it was an election year. You don't fight the D.A.s or the sheriffs during an election. Those guys are demigods on the bayou."

Louisiana is far from the only state using its justice apparatus as a profiteering scam. The State of Missouri has been using its criminal code to cover annual budget shortfalls for years. It costs the same as Ivy League tuition to put someone up at Rikers Island in New York. Some blocks in Brooklyn cost the state of New York over a million dollars a year.

In Louisiana, after the governor gutted all of the substantive provisions of the bills, Bobby and everyone else that had spent the last year poring over them lost it. "I'm telling my supervisors. 'We have to go public with this.'

But if Vera went public, Louisiana would never trust them or work with them again, his supervisors told him. Other states would hear about it and follow suit. They said, "I know you're frustrated but this is just the way things are and we can't do anything about it."

He swore. A lot. He creatively swore. I gave him a moment.

"Anywhere we're getting paid to do this work we're going to encounter the same dynamic. You can get a paycheck, or you can tell the truth, but never both."

Keep in mind, also, that this experience coincided with Vera's legal department telling him to shut down the fees and fines project in New York, and also with stop and frisk spiraling out of control across the street at City Hall. Hundreds of thousands of people who had done nothing wrong were being stopped and searched by police.

"We're all just sort of sitting quietly by, watching, thinking, 'This is so illegal. This is so messed up.' But again, we're not doing anything about it, and I realize I'm wasting my time. We're censored on multiple fronts, rendered impotent because of the way the justice funding paradigm is structured. This was not how I envisioned my life, or my career. I took an oath to protect the Constitution. I swore to never stand by while gross abuses of law and justice happened in front of me, and yet here I was doing exactly that. This was not justice. It was justice delayed. Justice never. Justice one day out of the year and injustice raging everywhere else all of the other days."

He quit.

Again.

He felt pissed and aimless. He went out to New Mexico with some money saved while at Vera. Outside Taos there was a little town called Arroyo Seco.

"There was something about that land that was alive. The Land of Enchantment, they call it."

He'd wanted to have a meaningful life, to contribute. "All my life I'd been led to believe that the enemy was certain people and places and things. In reality that's not what was going on. It was all a lie."

He keeps asking himself if you can do more in life than merely change things on a personal level.

"I took a dozen classes in law school that taught you that if systems were broken, you use the legal and political apparatus to fix them. But now, after working in the system all these years, I'm wondering if that's possible. Whether our current justice-for-profit paradigm is so inherently flawed that… I don't know… I don't really have an answer."

"Before I left Vera, I scoured the archives and realized: it's not just gun violence. It's all been solved. We knew how to solve mass incarceration thirty, forty years ago. We knew education programs and job training programs worked, and have worked effectively for years. The data backs this up — investments in people prevent recidivism. But once jurisdictions implement these policies and prison populations fall off, they realize employees will be laid off and infrastructure decommissioned. They panic because the people who staff these facilities are unionized. They vote, make phone calls, canvass during elections. There's a huge political cost if you implement programs that work because it will put thousands of well-connected, well-salaried cops, court officers, clerks, judges, and lawyers out of jobs."

Do any jurisdictions make the right call?

"There's an example in Texas called 'Right On Crime.' A while back Texas closed a bunch of prisons while reducing crime. For years people highlighted Texas as a national model of justice reinvestment. Tina Rosenberg, the same author who wrote about our program in Boston, wrote about it several times. And yet, here we are with a report out of U.T. Austin showing Texas has already rolled back many of its gains."

"Take Massachusetts, for example, the allegedly 'data-driven state' of Harvard, MIT, Northeastern, Tufts. Its inmate population has been going down every year for the last ten years while its annual corrections budget has steadily increased.

Not only that, but they're actually cutting all of the education and job incentive programs proven to prevent recidivism at the same time. It's a complete farce."

Back in New Mexico, he reads up on his history. A book called Parting the Waters, by Taylor Branch, rocks his world.

"Here I am thinking the only way to solve these problems is through courts, and political systems, and yet there are far more effective solutions to these problems that have been around for decades – no, centuries. Nonviolent alternatives have been used to shame power actors when they abuse civilians and communities. Financial boycotts have worked time and again, for example. The problem is not a lack of solutions – it's a lack of people willing to step outside the system and utilize them because there's no money in it.

"At every baseball game, hockey game, football game, fair, concert, carnival, rodeo, and car race, we talk about how great our country is. How we're imbued with this brave, revolutionary spirit, how our Constitution is sacred bedrock, how the amendments, our rights, our liberties, our justice for all, are sacrosanct.

"And yet we're failing to keep our word – miserably. Our go-to response as a society is to wait five to ten years and then file a lawsuit because that's how we all get paid. In the meantime, millions upon millions of people's lives are being harmed."

Bobby wondered if his friends, family, and colleagues knew that proven ways to stop these abuses of law and justice existed, so he came home and tried to rally his people into planning some actions that succeeded in the past.

In Parting the Waters lobby-ins or sit-in worked repeatedly. A crowd occupied a state building and kept it from conducting its daily business. One of our nation's first successful sit-ins happened in Worcester, Massachusetts — Bobby's birthplace, coincidentally — when a group of angry civilians blockaded the King's courts.

"I asked them to march to Florida's Sanford Criminal Justice Center and do a similar action after Trayvon Martin was killed. Surround the courthouse so they can't conduct business. And when we get arrested and released we will get right back in line. Say on a national level: there are consequences if you break the law when a civilian gets killed. We'll shut down your courthouse and municipal building for as long as it takes to get justice."

Their response?

"Had a high school friend tell me he puked in his mouth when he read my email. I said I was gonna go and they all told me I was an asshole, that they weren't coming. So now I'm wondering, 'Should I still go, even if I'm alone?'"

After several weeks of introspection — no late nights, no drinking, meditating and praying: "If you're there — something other than what I can see or feel or hear — guide whatever it is I'm about to do. Please. Be with me."

To this day he wonders…

"I was very clearly feeling this thing — whatever it might be — telling me, 'Just go. Just do it. Don't worry about the other stuff. Just go…'"

Bobby rounded up friends from Boston, who marched a few miles, and said, "To Florida. The clothes on my back and a toothbrush. Nothing else has worked, so let's try this. If I make it on the kindness of strangers, I make it. If I don't, I don't."

One of his friends — Rachel Moo — shared his Facebook post with a class she taught in Dorchester on nonviolent resistance. On his way through Dorchester, he stopped in and met with her second graders. That day, the class made a bunch of signs and marched with him down the block.

In the aftermath of the Boston Marathon bombing, one of the signs saying, "No more hurting people. PEACE," showed up in President Obama's speech.

All Bobby had in mind that day was the joy of the class. (The attack was a year away.) He walked nineteen miles to Brockton's YMCA, where he met a local pastor and stayed with her family.

The next day, 23 miles to Providence.

On his way out, the authorities in Sanford charged George Zimmerman. His friend, Mardi, bought him a train ticket home.

Boston.com wrote up Bobby's "amazing experience." Few came, but he felt vindicated because it was as if he'd gone with the grain of the universe for once, "Everyone's on social media screaming at each other and yet I met a bunch of loving strangers in real life who let me stay in their homes, have dinner with them, no questions asked. Sixty miles into the unknown, guy charged on the third day, and I came home. This notion of go, don't worry about the rest seemed to be valid. It's like it was saying you might not be the thing that causes an indictment, but if you put yourself on the line for what is right all of the details will work out. Don't worry about it. Just go."

The first week back he wondered if it was real, or just a function of being well-connected – white privilege, if you will? Coming off the heels of Parting the Waters, drawing from that well of Benedictine concern for a just and equitable society, making it 60 miles with no problems after his friends told him he'd freeze to death in a ditch for nothing, he was surprised when, instead of remarking on the fact that he made it, and an indictment issued, his friends and family criticized him:

"How can you invite us to walk to Florida? We can't walk to Florida. It's way too far."

"Alright, I'll do something local, then, without so much walking. That way you can come."

Parting the Waters features a lobby-in where men, women, and children occupied downtown Birmingham. Those denied the right to vote shut down businesses around the courthouse. Soon, local business owners were calling the mayor and telling him to give the protestors what they wanted because they were losing money. The hardware store, Woolworth's, the movie theater – they all closed when protestors descended.

That in mind, Bobby said, "Let's occupy City Hall like the residents of Birmingham until the mayor pledges to end the illegality of stop and frisk."

He invited everyone. Again everyone called him a moron. He showed up on the appointed day and time. No one else did. Again. He sat down on a bench in Battery Park, unsure about what to do, hoping someone, anyone, would show. Didn't happen.

A lobby-in is a strategic action that requires a large number of people to work. So he summoned whatever it was he thought he might be hearing during his march.

"Whatever you are, if you're real, if you were really there before…"

Again, he heard it or maybe felt it repeating, "Just go. Don't worry."

He continued, laughing, "Now, I don't know what this means: 'Go.' I'm like, 'Okay, where? And, more importantly, to do what?'" He worked out the details while shivering on the bench.

His friend, Shaun, had made him a stencil to spray-paint a message on the t-shirts and hoodies of participants as they arrived. It said NYPD GET YOUR HANDS OFF ME. He had it with him, and two cans of spray-paint.

"I'm angry at my family and friends for not showing because I see them out there every Fourth of July lighting fireworks and eating burgers, only now it's go-time, time to defend the document we're supposedly lighting bottle rockets for, and they're telling me I'm some kind of asshole for trying to get them to do something about it. So I decide to play a game of chicken with them: 'demand the Mayor stop breaking the law or watch me get arrested 20 times in a row and get sent to jail.'

Mind you, this is New York City. The most prestigious City Hall in America sits at the crossroads of one of the nation's busiest intersections in Lower Manhattan — the base of the Brooklyn Bridge. Bobby assumes this means he'll be able to start his arrest, release, repeat cycle easily.

"I spray-paint all of the gates at City Hall. I'm five feet away from the guards. I can see them watching the cameras that are recording everything."

If you see on the video, a police go cart pulls up, lights flashing. There's a transport wagon in the distance, two cops pass. He spray paints the stencil right in front of all of it.

"I felt invisible, and not just because I'm white, and not just because I'm privileged, and not just because I'm wearing a suit. I mean, I'm right there in the picture, standing a couple of feet directly in front of the guard. I see him watching the different camera monitors, and yet for some reason he can't see me. A cop pulls up, looks right at me, and then drives away, like I'm not there. It's just plain weird. I paint six different gates, all of it on camera, as cars, taxis, police vans, and go-carts are whizzing by, and, well… nothing. I'm literally trying to be seen…and I can't."

He went home, called some reporters, told them someone tagged graffiti on City Hall.

"Fox News reported on it in the morning."

Proof in hand, he planned to turn himself in when he woke up. He donned his suit for court, posted a blog admitting guilt, and signed a letter of confession for the guards. He went down to the same gate he painted the night before to give this document to the guards and turn himself in.

Showing his I.D., he handed the letter over to the guard.

The guard took a picture of the I.D. and made a call. Then hangs up and says, "Make an appointment."

"Well can you at least drop my letter off to the mayor?"

The guard agrees, calls to check, then says he still needs an appointment.

"I can't drop off a letter for the mayor at City Hall?"

"No, you need an appointment."

At home he blogs about that incident, admitting it again, basically waiting for the police to knock on his door at this point.

"It's deafening silence. My friends and family are all in this awkward position, devouring every word I'm posting, but refusing to comment or engage."

This happens for five more days. Three more times Bobby returns, on one occasion going so far as to bring a reporter with him, but every time the guards at the gate turn him away.

That week Manhattan Criminal Court held a trial of activists who were arrested for protesting stop and frisk in front of a Harlem precinct. Daily Bobby attends and on day five, the judge declares them guilty and sentences them. The prosecutor in Bobby seethed at the verdict because the entire case was based on hypothetical, rather than actual, evidence: not a single person had testified that they had been prevented from entering the precinct or conducting other official business due to the protest.

Bobby stood up in the courtroom, put his hands on his head, and announced that he was sitting in and refusing to leave the courtroom in protest. He hoped the observers present in the gallery would join him and refuse to leave, an impromptu lobby-in of sorts, but the court officers moved in and slowly filed everyone out.

Bobby was taken to central booking.

And he realized getting arrested over and over would never suffice.

"My mother's this devout Evangelical Christian saying, 'Well what are they—' meaning the people being mistreated by the police '— 'going to do for themselves?' It made me want to scream. I mean, it was just so gross. I'm in central booking seeing people coming in with broken wrists, multiple Taser burns, lumps sticking out of the sides of their heads, and I'm looking around at the other white guys in the cell with me, asking them, 'did they treat you like that?' and we're all like, 'no', not a single one of us had so much as a scratch on our wrists. These horrific abuses of law and person were happening (cases like Jateik Reed, Ramarley Graham, and so many others), they violated everything our country claimed to stand for, and yet everyone I knew in my life kept making excuses about how it wasn't their responsibility to get involved."

Bobby mentions how similar acts set up the Holocaust:

"The police in Italy and Germany started giving Jewish residents hell, and the general public stood around and watched. That's where it starts. The cops doing this crap and getting away with it, and knowing they can get away with it because people in the majority aren't going to do a damn thing to get in the way other than file a lawsuit, which gives them years to keep breaking the law and hurting people in the meantime."

He mentioned the unarmed eighteen-year-old Israel Hernandez getting tazed to death. He reminded me of the Nashville twenty-eight-year-old Tory Sanders who died from pepper spray and stun guns in a Southeast Missouri jail while passing through and asking for an attorney. This state sponsored lynching combined with the seventy-seven-year-old woman who had a heart attack from the brutality of the same sheriff's handcuffing prompted the ACLU to issue its first ever travel advisory for the state of Missouri. Bobby reminded me of the timeline of police shooting twelve-year-old Tamir Rice, and later Sandra Bland, who died in police custody. When you consider the whole list, the 1162 killed last year and the 677 killed already this year, it baffles the mind, particularly when you consider the ages (infants and elderly), genders, means of extrajudicial execution, and the bodycams, dashcams and witness videos showing so many unarmed civilians being killed for nothing.

"How do they not see it? I spent another few days deep in meditation: 'You, whatever thing I think I hear harping in my ear all the time, what now? Should I call the whole thing off? Save what little face I have left? I'm clearly not getting anywhere, getting only bad feedback from everyone. The New York Post is mocking me, my friends and family are ignoring me — nobody gives a rip.

But something just keeps saying, "Go.' Go, go, go. Stop worrying about it and go…'"

Again, he has no idea what this means, but he's furious at how none of his people are engaging, "I have to try and do something to change their minds...

"I wanted to know what's the one thing I can do that will force — literally force — them to engage?"

He goes down to City Hall. By himself. Eats no food. Drinks no water. "I write it up on social media, my blog: 'On May 14, I'm going to march around City Hall without food or water until I collapse or the mayor ends stop and frisk."

Below he wrote the mayor's office number and mailing address.

"You think you're so great and patriotic and moral, well prove it."

Bobby's friends and family said change takes time. He's being too impatient. Reminds me of Martin Luther King's words from Letter from a Birmingham Jail:

I have almost reached the regrettable conclusion that the Negro's great stumbling block in his stride toward freedom is not the White Citizen's Counciler or the Ku Klux Klanner, but the white moderate, who is more devoted to "order" than to justice. [Who say we are in too much of a hurry and that "these things take time"]

Bobby said, "For me it's twelve years. For others, decades. Others still, centuries. How much time do we need? Joel pointed out earlier, Lance, that I shouldn't say we didn't make any progress. One of the guys went to college. But I'm measuring progress not necessarily as systemic change. We can only influence our own circles of people. My circle's super wealthy, white, privileged, educated. For me it seemed like the needle wasn't moving with them. I'm trying so hard to change their minds and I'm meeting constant opposition, constant reaffirmation of the same flawed narrative that drove this thing. They keep recapitulating it like robots. 'Well these people are dangerous criminals, they need to la la la.'"

Two minutes after he announced his intentions, Rachel Moo replied, "No! That's the day you're coming to Boston to march with my class!"

He amended the day to Wednesday, not Monday.

"Two hours after I change it to Wednesday she calls me back and says, 'Uh, hey, did you buy your ticket?' I say, 'Yeah, why?' She says, 'Get a refund. The parents found out who you are and they don't want you to come.'"

Rachel had reposted everything on social media.

"She's one of the few people who supported me through all this, right? My friend Mardi was another one. Rachel's Asian. Mardi's black. None of my white friends, save three or four, Christina, Glenn, Leah, and Shaun, supported me at all. My family certainly didn't."

His trip to Boston canceled, he decided to stick with Wednesday, and this is a detail that turns out to be very, very significant later on.

Again, he enters into a period of deep contemplation and wonders if the thing telling him 'Go' is a delusion. Were his friends right?

Was he mentally ill?

If he committed to this food and water strike, he needed to follow it through to the end, come what may. An ambulance might not arrive in time. Following through could mean no voice had spoken at all. He might die over an illusion, a figment.

He chose a food and water strike because he thinks hunger strikes are too long for modern-day attention spans.

"Two-to-three days before I reach my body's limit. If I'm nonstop marching, a day and a half. That's gonna put a lot of attention on my demands, and a lot of pressure on the people who supposedly care about me, to take action to help me meet these demands today, rather than in a month or two."

He went down on Wednesday morning and no one he invited showed. He walked around City Hall while former friends and colleagues showed up to work at Vera, which shamed him. "I felt like the biggest loser on the planet, to be honest. Couldn't even get a single freaking person to come with me."

"Screw it. I start doing laps around City Hall by myself with a 'March Against Stop and Frisk' sign. This tall black guy with a camouflage military rucksack comes up and says, 'Get against the wall!' He starts patting me down and says, 'I'm just kidding, my name's Jesse. I'm from the Stop Stop and Frisk crew, just wanted to hear more about why you're doing this…'"

Jesse Hall was the first who came. He became Bobby's "guardian angel." He held Bobby's coat, a bottle of water in case Bobby collapsed, but Bobby refused. Mid-eighty-degree weather and Bobby's fading fast, sweating out fluids he'd hoped would last two days.

As the day progresses, all these people he doesn't know start showing up.

New York activists.

They called his plan to walk nonstop through the night and into the morning "dangerous. Cops and others are saying things on social media. Have Jesse go home with you tonight and come back first thing in the morning."

They stop at 10pm. Go home. Jesse spends the night. Bobby wakes up at 6am. "I had this sudden searing pain wake me from a deep sleep."

He didn't know what it was.

But he was up.

"Might as well go marching. Turns out the day before, a federal judge had certified a pending class action suit against the City of New York after months and months of deliberating. She said if the City didn't fix stop and frisk, she would. The journalist that night from Courthouse News Service— Adam Klasfield — said, 'You're not gonna believe this.'"

The stop and frisk ruling was scathing. It demanded an immediate fix.

Bobby wondered if this was his out.

But reporters tracked down NYPD Commissioner Ray Kelly the night of the ruling and he defiantly doubled down on stop and frisk. Bobby and Jesse shrugged and headed back out, unsure how long he'd make it through the second day of marching.

"My joints, my hips, everything is aching. I'm grinding my teeth into paste because I'm so hungry."

He's in no condition to march, starting to totter with sloppy steps. Jesse watched the curb in case Bobby fell towards oncoming traffic, tried to force him to drink water "like my mom or something," but Bobby refused.

"We're going back and forth about it, laughing."

Around noon, City Hall's guards begin to pay more attention to them. Bobby's letter to the mayor called the program illegal, wrong, a lie "there's three decades of data that show there are programs the city could be using to stop gun violence instead of trampling rights and putting kids in jail. And I know the mayor knows this because the Bloomberg School of Public Health at John Hopkins is named after him."

That January, the school with the Mayor's name on it issued a report evaluating the same program model Boston used, but in Baltimore. They found HUGE program-related reductions in youth gun violence.

"Here he is calling himself the 'data mayor' while trotting his police commissioner out to lie to the entire country about what the data says."

Bobby's letter said follow the data or I'll die on your stoop. And it's not gonna look good. Cause it's Bloomberg's own data. Reporters swarm the area, looking for interviews on the subject because of the judge's ruling the day before, and it's starting to make the guards uneasy.

A reporter tells Bobby the mayor has just called an unscheduled press conference. Reporters rush the front gate, to attend, but can't get in because it's full.

They rush across the street with their gear and cameras. Jesse and Bobby follow, curious.

"Bill de Blasio steps out of his office (then-Public Advocate, not yet Mayor) and takes the podium. He announces that Ray Kelly and Michael Bloomberg have 'this very morning committed one of the biggest flip-flops in city history.'"

After defiantly defending stop and frisk the day prior, the city announced a set of reforms that conceded to use COMPSTAT (the NYPD's data system) to review and reform NYPD's illegal stop and frisk practices.

Bobby's under the sun about to collapse.

Jesse smiles, yanks out a bottle of water and calmly hands it over as if that was the plan all along.

Bobby chugs it "faster than I've ever chugged anything. And, man, it's better than the best champagne I've ever had. The best thing I'd ever tasted. Somehow, someway, I'm walking away from this action under my own power."

Is he claiming to have performed a miracle? To have personally ended stop and frisk in New York City?

"Look, I'm not gonna sit here and tell you I'm the reason stop and frisk ended. Obviously I'm not the reason. But look at the numbers: since that day, stop and frisk went from 685,000 a year to less than 30,000. We're by no means out of the woods — they've morphed it into other things like weed arrests, quality of life arrests, turnstile jumping, gang raids, and such. But that being said, following this — still, to this day, five years later — not a single person in my family, not one of my friends, not one of my colleagues — NO ONE has said, 'We called you an asshole and mentally ill, but it's pretty remarkable that you survived. You marched to Florida and three days later the guy was arrested. You tried to get yourself arrested and were invisible for a week. You put your life on the line like a complete moron and, yet, two days later, against all of the odds, you got exactly what you demanded and walked away unharmed.'

What do we do as a species when the dark underside of our nature shows its face in the form of illegal policies, false arrests, mass incarceration, police killing? How should we respond as citizens?

"When I was doing these actions five years ago, I don't think people were ready to look at the state of the world and say 'we're in crisis.' I was seeing firsthand how dysfunctional it was every day because I was deep in the nitty gritty of the criminal justice system, but we, as a citizenry, weren't ready to hear it.

"But now everyone is saying, 'Oh my God, we've reached a crisis point. What can we do? During all of these actions something big, and powerful, beyond my scope of vision, seemed to be saying, "Go and put your privilege, your life, and your body on the line, and don't worry about the rest."

"Before we make another phone call, before we try to get another candidate elected, before we punch another Nazi in the face, we need to figure out what this thing is and figure out how we can use it to get in the way of injustice together."

"This might sound unrealistic, or naïve, but look at our political system right now. These clowns can't even figure out how to repeal health care legislation. Thirty years of data showing us how to stop recidivism, and yet we're cutting the programs that work while law enforcement budgets soar into the billions. Look at our military, the War On Terror: we've spent $6 trillion in the last 16 years – $20 million a day – and the terrorism index shows terror incidents going up and up and up every year. The glaciers are melting, temps are rising, and we can't even agree on whether or not to stop driving cars.

"And you can't just blame it on conservatives, either. Baltimore, Boston, Chicago – these are the most liberal cities in the country allowing young people to die while ignoring 30 years of data. Our political system is never going to get us there. More violence, more guns, more wars won't either. There's got to be another way. If something big, and powerful, is calling us forth, and it wants to work miracles on our behalf, wants to use us to bend the arc of this universe towards justice, we need to get serious about summoning it. But right now we bicker with each other.

"When I did all of these actions, everyone I knew doubted me. They told me I was insane, that I was an idiot, that I was going to die for nothing. Only in each and every instance, this thing came through and had my back. Each and every time it spared me, kept its word, faithfully sorted out the details."

Bobby convinces me we could live in a world where we don't have a thing to fear. Wouldn't that be nice? What if you never had to be afraid again? What if all of the news reports and flashing lights and doors breaking down is an illusion to keep us afraid and indoors and paying for endless and unnecessary police raids and S.W.A.T. equipment — guns and tanks and choppers — that, statistically, year after year, fail to prevent the very thing we're told they prevent?

And if we really want to never be afraid again, then why choose to remain so? Because it would take courage — much more than mayoral, congressional, judicial, and political courage — to make programs like Bobby's permanent in the teeth of juggernaut police departments and those who make their living off of the cycle of prison and death.

Of course, to do that, we'd have to get rid of the fences and walls and battering rams. To do that, we'd have to get involved in our neighbors' lives.

To do that, we'd have to stop being afraid, set down our guns and our fear-mongering news bulletins and literally love our literal neighbor as ourselves instead of buying cross-stitch and reusable shopping bags and black-painted wooden boards sporting that phrase. The courage to love our neighbor rather than kill them or throw them in some dungeon to rot?

It's almost as if we've known the solution all along.

You get forgiven if the convict does because, as Nathan said to David, *you **are** the man*. YOU are as guilty as anyone else. That's why the classical confession predicated on the book of James starts *mea culpa*. Through my fault. My bad. You take responsibility for your wrongs. It's why when the London Times asked literary voices from around the world to write essays on what's wrong with the world, HG Wells and Shaw and all sorts of voices chimed in with luminous essays on where the world went wrong. But their buddy and dueling partner Chesterton wrote a seven word response:

> *Dear Sirs,*
> *I am.*
> *Sincerely,*
> *G.K. Chesterton*

Self defense, self righteousness, is just easier.

It's easier for the father of the murdered daughter to forget how he may have neglected her or murdered her in his mind during a particularly difficult season of discipline. It's easier for the mother of the sexually abused child to forget how she may have emotionally or spiritually abused him prior. It's easier for the victim of grand theft auto to forget how he mentally stole time away from his mom through a psychopathic need to gaslight her. We forget, so easily, the passing thoughts and acts and words that condemn us.

And so we perpetuate the cycle of death. The abused, abuse. Victims of theft steal away years of the life of others. The myth of redemptive violence hangs over all, leaving the eye-for-an-eye world blind and toothless, no one stops to consider the long chain of history and only seeing their own personal wrongs.

It helps us ignore the convict once they've actually become penitent. Once they actually *beg* for forgiveness. It's just easier to lock human beings up like animals and pretend I'm fine, you're fine, everything is fine. Our country is quite good at that: we incarcerate magnitudes of order more people than anyone else in the world. Comes from being a guilt / innocence culture: we tend to think only one person is to blame. When that stops being Jesus, we end up being scape goats litigating scape goats. But if we blame shift long enough, <u>no one takes any responsibility for anything</u>. Or, worse, if we shift *all* of the blame to one person, everyone else can wash their hands of responsibility. It's the Guy Fawkes thing: people still die outside the city gate, it's just *after* Jesus so we don't even get the benefit of the God outside the gate when we decide to return to witch burnings (which, by the way, was invented by alchemists and not Christians, so it's not even a Christian thing at the root). You end in a scenario with way too many prosecutors and the most prosecuted end up becoming the most imprisoned. Remove those entities from government and church, and you end with literal corporations whose job it is to get more and more people into prison and keep them there. And since that class of people *can't vote*, they can't fix the problems they see *from the inside*. So we become perpetually blind to this Gehenna we've created.

We refuse to stare into the abyss of the very oubliettes we dig. Particularly when we get paid — or voted into office — in order to dig them.

That's what people mean by "the prison industrial complex": it's a factory and caged animals once known as your neighbor — the one God tells you to love — come hot off the conveyer belt. Sometimes literally in death penalty states. Hot off the press. And just as dead on the page. Your bad. My bad.

And it ends up rippling into the homeless shelter system, as we've already seen with Will. It ends up rippling into the refugee system, as we saw with the myth of redemptive violence that left the Palestinian Christian's home playing host to the Zionist and Muslim trading rockets.

Originally, I had a letter from an ex-convict in this book. I once co-wrote a piece for the World Series edition of Poker Pro while he was still in prison. The piece was on bankroll management in prison — oranges and stamps, mostly. The letter he'd written for this book was asking for forgiveness for him and the clients under his care who *did* commit the crime, *did* serve their time as little more than animals in cages (something no human being should be subjected to: we don't decrease dehumanization by responding with more dehumanization). The piece ended "Forgive us. Forgive those who forgive us too."

He took it out.

Because even though he had graduated from a New York law firm, he *still* has to keep his head down still because of his former conviction — and expired probation — for a sin and crime he committed two decades ago, one he's healed from and changed.

In the middle of his prison sentence, I and a few other friends wrote him letters. Everyone had abandoned him: for good reason, that's the thing. The sin of bitterness *always* comes with good reasons — you have a *good reason* to be bitter, but bitterness is a root that will destroy not them, but *you*. The only antidote — I mean the only one — is the sacrament of reconciliation, restoration, forgiveness. You have *good reason* to neglect grace to the least of these convicts. Or the sick. Or the hungry. Bitter people always have reasons. Even some of the best dudes at the Jackie Gleason depot had *good reason* for refusing to help Will. You know who else has good reasons? People who already have everything and want to keep it and therefore refuse to share it.

Yet Jesus says, "Forgive us our trespasses as we forgive those who trespass against us." He said *if we don't* forgive, *we won't* be forgiven.

It's the same logic of the least of these passage. The same logic of the judgment passage in the sermon on the mount. Or Romans 1 *&* 2.

This dude didn't just damage one person's life. One ministry. One forwarding agency. He damaged *my* reputation because I had, in my ignorance, been *passing his lies* on to people about what he was doing simply because I took his lies as face-value truth. It ruined *my* relationship with folks — still does when they find out I still see him, still associate with him, still receive his recommendation on certain job related issues. That hurt in ways I'll never be able to articulate. But could I forgive him for his sins against that person in specific, that org, that forwarding agency, the broader faith and creative and governmental community? For sinning against me in particular? Would I buy him a beer?

Better question:

How oh how oh how does Jesus still associate with me? Still forgive me? Still want to hang out with me when I deserve ten times worse than my friend?

I often tell people who say it's *so great* that I baptized a friend who was sort of a regional manager for crack dealers — like FBI-bust level amounts of coke — that he's a better man than me. I baptized *my better* and he repented and stopped dealing.

I'm no hero. I get this stuff wrong all the time. But I (and sometimes Tara) wrote a letter to the first convict almost every three days at peak. He told me horror stories: far worse that his crime was done to him in prison. Did he deserve it? At what point in the process after we crossed past the eye for an eye line did he *keep* deserving it? Or keep deserving it *now* after he has done his time and parole? Because Jesus rebukes eye for eye thinking: predominantly because of how guilty we all are and also because of how the nature of judgment sets us up as God over our fellow in such a way that we end up ourselves judged by those we judge. It's a cycle of hypocrisy and never ends. Either we make ourselves out to be God, the judge, or we make someone else out to be judge. Jesus says don't cast your pearls to swine on that front, don't give the sacred right of divine judgment up to dogs — whether yourself or someone else. Rather pray. Ask God for what you need. Seek. Knock. Because the Father gives good things to his children: bread, not a stone; fish, not a snake. And therefore the best we can do is to treat other people the way we'd want to be treated in their position. To forgive them and leave the conviction in their lap where it will fester, where it will start to work on them a Godly sorrow rather than merely as the sorrow of man. The cycle of hypocrisy never ends… Unless… He wrote this letter to me halfway through:

> *I pray for God to provide work for me on the outside, as so many of these guys say finding work is impossible for us. I know something will be made available, but I catch myself attaching a clause to the prayer. I still have such a strong desire to do something big or fun. Writing or filmmaking or whatever. This feels greedy and causes me to doubt. So I believe God will bless me with work but I don't believe he'll give me the kind of work I really want. It's that Baptist guilt I've always had that I should suffer more for my sins.*
>
> *Any advice, Lance?*

> *...All I want to do is not sin, not commit any more crimes, never disappoint my parents again, and work incredibly hard to build up the culture of a small community. I want to be a faithful man of prayer and study my bible and grow wise and old. Not even famous anymore.*
>
> *Lots of murderers and bankrobbers in here and even an honest to goodness terrorist, but still snitches and sex criminals are the most hated.*

His letters to me are filled with back and forth studies on the book of 1 John and James and the gospels. He led one of the weirdest bible studies I've ever heard of while in the pen, yet still saw transformation in the art thief who dealt paintings to Robin Williams and in the serial killer who used knives and in the honest-to-goodness terrorist. He did correspondence courses for bible college credit from the very ministry that used to rent us our house in Joplin. Played correspondence chess with me *one letter at a time* with my board upstairs and him keeping track on paper. And I was able to pitch some of his articles and get one published in the World Series of Poker edition of Poker Pro. We co-wrote it: *Poker in the Pokey*. I did what I could to encourage him towards the light. I am one man and a failing one. It's not enough.

He didn't have support when he left. He didn't have a community to restore him as he *begged* at the end of that letter we removed from this book. So when he got ahold of Hitchens and Dawkins, are you surprised to learn he's an atheist now of the pop culture variety?

In the face of that, a nurse friend tried to shame me for accepting his public review of my work. A relative tried to tell me he didn't do the hard work of repentance, as if the relative knew the whole story (when all his only info came from that conversation). The list goes on: folks not only can't forgive him, *they can't forgive me for forgiving him.* His ending was right: forgive them, forgive those *who forgive them.* What if instead of all of that you and a few more Christians had come to visit him? Write him? What if you took the woman caught in adultery as your model: refusing to throw the first stone *if — and I mean truly if — you yourself have any guilt?* What if you had seen the humanity for which Jesus says, "This is me too"?

Not the criminal. Not the heinous act of violence he committed. And I do mean heinous: I cannot tell you the number of conversations we've had about that, which led to him really and truly admitting how wrong it was. What if you saw the human being broken beyond repair without the forgiveness he begs to receive? Begs. I know forty-year tenured Christians who have never *begged* God for forgiveness.

Is that what Jesus meant by one sinner who comes to repentance when ninety-nine "righteous" don't?

Cause even after all he did, he's not a chimp and he's not a demon. Some might argue he was possessed of a demon, that he acted like a chimp, and therefore deserves to be exorcised as one, caged as one. But friend! Either our war is *not* against flesh and blood. Or it is. Either we believe free range is more humane or we don't. If it isn't, then Jesus says, "What grace you've done unto the *least* convict, you've done unto me" as often as he says "If anyone harms these little ones of mine, it would be better if a large milestone were hung around his neck and he were thrown in the sea." If it is, then why even talk about anything spiritual ever? Why talk about forgiveness? We at least give chimps terrariums these days. We give fish aquariums. It at least *looks* like their native environs.

This convict was a little one too, you see. Something was done to him. And grace wasn't received. And he ended up a convict. At what point do we stop the cycle? Either forgiveness and grace are radically offered to a man who has faced the horror of the violence he did or they aren't.

If they aren't, then you're not a Christian. Straight up. You're a Muslim. Or maybe a Mormon. You're just like everybody else who bolsters the Pax Romana with "family values" so the American Imperial cult can declare war on some black and brown nation and bomb the living daylights out of their babies in order for you to eat your meals with your 2.5 kids in quiet and loneliness. You can watch as a dispassionate voyeur while other human beings get slaughtered in the arena for your entertainment. Some of them *are martyrs*, you just won't know it until Jesus returns.

It's not about forgiveness at that point. It's just about status quo verses chaos. That's small time. Come join the big time. Stop sending people down river. Bring them back upstream to the fountain of life and youth.

What if Someone Takes Advantage of Me?

It's an honest question: what if you get abused? What if you become a doormat? What if someone takes advantage of you?

For starters, I'm not advocating for erasing the clear boundaries of your personhood. Even within the perichoretic dance of the Trinity, the persons retain personhood. If you're emotionally enmeshing with people; if you're codependent; if you're saying things often like "you made me feel" and blaming your issues on your personality profile (read: horoscope) and taking a completely passive approach to your life — perhaps flirting and flying from one lost cause to another in order to make yourself feel superior... the list goes on, but if you're doing these and more (not to mention several abusive cases in the b-cluster personality types — borderline personality disorder, HPD, narcissism, psychopathy, sociopathy) you can actually end up *taking advantage* of the least of these. It's an extremely nuanced point but it needs to be made: I'm advocating neither for you to be blindly abused nor for you to blindly abuse others simply to prop up your own feelings.

How do you know?

Can you ever?

There are really two postures that do not fit the life of Jesus. One is passivity and the other is violence. One is that of the victimized and the other is that of the jaded abuser. They exist on a continuum quite often, depending on the chronology of any given life. Hurt people hurt people: we emotionally, mentally, spiritually, physically, and sexually abuse *because we were emotionally, mentally, spiritually, physically, and sexually abused*. Specifically we do it because we doubt and believe we're the sort of creature that dies permanently in the second death. That even dies so permanently in the first death. We do it because we're atheists. We think God's dead and so we try to survive as long as we can.

And you can tell that by the way people talk about creation these days: if you think creation means God created the world in six days, that he used certain physical materials, that he created an efficient chain of cause and effect — like dominoes — so that you could come to exist, you don't understand creation. All of that may be useful, but it doesn't explain why a Tesla Model X exists in this moment. And this moment. And this moment. Instantaneous being is what traditional theists mean. Even a renowned preacher like Tim Keller gets this wrong in his *Reason for God* and I lost a ton of respect for him when I realized he didn't understand basic ideas of contingency. The donation of the Creator to creation means that if God removed his permission at any moment in any space from any thing or person, that thing or person would cease to exist. It's because *nothing* contains the cause of its being. If you don't understand that — if you don't understand the wonder that the book you hold, as a lonely object in nothingness, has *zero reason to exist right now outside of God saying, right now,* **BE** — then, functionally, you're an atheist.

And if you're trying to merely survive in that cosmic abyss, you're doubly an atheist — whether from passive hiding or violence, whether from being victimized or abusing.

"Survival is insufficient," says both Star Trek and *Station Eleven*.

Don't be an atheist in everything but name.

Don't lie to yourself and say that the only true reality is that you'll die and then, maybe, in the sweet by and by you'll go up to heaven. That's the way slaveowners talk, not you. That's the way Gnostic heretics talk, not you. You must stop domineering to merely survive. Only the people who truly believe in resurrection break the cycle.

On the side of the victimized, people become victims when they do not realize real malice exists in the world. If they don't believe it exists in them, whenever they inevitably do something atrocious (for all have sinned and fallen short of the glory of God), they develop PTSD and constantly relive the awful thing they did. "Triggering" in this sense is actually triggering *the weapon* that they have become. The other is trauma done to them they — almost always — did not expect or reckon. "Triggering" this actually often causes them to experience the abuse and retraumatize. Again it's naive, but it's naive for *other people*. The sort of silent response is "well what do you expect? People are awful."

This song of innocence, once shattered, often leads to songs of experience. More like songs of the shattered and songs of the shatterer. The masochist, once he learns what awful things can be done to him, tries to recapture naïveté and ritually suffers abuse. The sadist, once she learns what awful things she can do, truest to purge her own innocence fully by ritually abusing. On the other side of the victimized lives the victimizer, hurting because he was hurt. They start out passive, they end up violent.

There's a third way.

I do not want you to be naive, my brothers and sisters, in knowing that the world can abuse you. Nor that you can abuse. Indeed, many of the least of these are least because they're the runts of the litter: the one who gets the least food, least clean water, least shelter, least healthcare, least clean and fitting clothing, least dignity in prison. Often *the abused* end up in these categories and sometimes even because they became abusers: it's a statistical truism that the at least a third of molesters were molested. That Donald Trump gaslit the entire world because his mother gaslit him. That the starving person becomes the hoarder and uses *thou shalt not steal* as justification for coveting: simply using the laws of property to legally take what's common to all — ocean, sky, oil beneath a small town — doesn't mean you aren't exploiting. That the homeless becomes the gentrifying real estate developer. That the refugee becomes the tyrant who displaces. In fact that last one is *precisely* the story of America. We are now King George. Puerto Rico, for instance, and Washington D.C. and Samoa experience precisely taxation without representation.

I'm not advocating for ignorance: you can get deeply, profoundly hurt when it comes to food and water and nakedness (or bodily autonomy) and sickness and shelter and freedom to roam. Surely sometimes, as in the case of the convict, you need a come-to-Jesus moment that takes facing the dragon within. *Mea culpa.*

But I'm also not advocating for a jadedness that does nothing. Or worse than nothing. Or who uses that jadedness as an excuse for tyranny with them as king, controller, manager. This is the person who talks about alpha males and alpha females. Anyone telling you humans have *real* hierarchies is an idiot. Like the sort of idiot the Proverbs warns us about. Humans aren't chimps and they aren't demons. The only people claiming humans have hierarchies are deluded by chimps and demons. Or, if they really believe that, why aren't they in submission to the only institution that (through inversion) has a legitimate moral claim to hierarchy: The Catholic Church? Chesterton once addressed this:

> There has fallen on earth for a token
> A god too great for the sky.
> He has burst out of all things and broken
> The bounds of eternity:
>
> Into time and the terminal land

He has strayed like a thief or a lover,
For the wine of the world brims over,
Its splendour is split on the sand.

Who is proud when the heavens are humble,
Who mounts if the mountains fall,
If the fixed stars topple and tumble
And a deluge of love drowns all-

Who rears up his head for a crown,
Who holds up his will for a warrant,
Who strives with the starry torrent,
When all that is good goes down?

For in dread of such falling and failing
The fallen angels fell
Inverted in insolence, scaling
The hanging mountain of hell:

But unmeasured of plummet and rod
Too deep for their sight to scan,
Outrushing the fall of man
Is the height of the fall of God.

Glory to God in the Lowest
The spout of the stars in spate-
Where thunderbolt thinks to be slowest
And the lightning fears to be late:

As men dive for sunken gem
Pursuing, we hunt and hound it,

The fallen star has found it
In the cavern of Bethlehem.

If they aren't in submission to the moral, intellectual, and aesthetic authority of the world — the Pope — they don't actually believe hierarchy exists. Or they think they — themselves — ARE the pope. And most churches, by the way they talk ahistorically of heretics, are run by little more than little popes. Little popes and little councils of cardinals without the credentials or the miracles or the intellectual horsepower to back it up. Both of those options make a mockery of hierarchical thinking and the person proportions it. And, ironically enough, the entire hierarchy of Christendom, when it is actually Christendom, is literally the opposite of hierarchy. It's an inverted race all the way down to Bethlehem. To wash the feet of Judas.

We forget that part of the towel and basin, you know. That it's not just that Jesus took on the form of a slave, as Paul said in Philippians: he took on the form of *Judas's slave*. We enter the basilica of the Christchild on our knees.

Everyone sits lonely atop the hierarchy of individualism. Everyone sits lonely at the bottom of the well of community. Anyone who calls themselves or refers to someone else as, for instance, an "alpha" not only doesn't understand themselves but doesn't understand the world. Alphas are for creatures that either throw feces or whisper lies and cause destruction, not good humans.

We found out in Jesus and the prophets and martyrs that hierarchies have zero legitimate power. They're made of communities playing pretend. Playing at ape or playing at demonic power. And that stage play is deadly. The only way to fix it is service. Not servant leadership. Service.

True power is word made flesh. The true icon of God is one of the names of Jesus. True power is first making new ideas, stretching the bounds of possible good ideas and making those possibilities into actual reality, science into art. Art and service.

It is, in fact, impossible to believe in consciousness and call us beasts. It is, in fact, impossible to believe in incarnation and call us demons. It's impossible, all around, to appeal to the hierarchies in demons and beasts as license for tyranny against those who abused you. Power isn't controlling or manipulating others. Just because you lost your innocence doesn't mean losing more or stealing the innocence of others is the way. You might say, "I see through that." I have relative who acts as if they see through everything and therefore take nothing — not even a watercolor painting — at face value. Descartes says once you start to doubt your *doubt* — to criticize your own *criticism* — you end up with nothing. C.S. Lewis says it this way:

> Perhaps, in the nature of things, analytical understanding must always be a basilisk which kills what it sees and only sees by killing. but if the scientists themselves cannot arrest this process before it reaches the common Reason

and kills that too, then someone else must arrest it. What I most fear is the reply that I am 'only one more' obscurantist, that this barrier, like all previous barriers set up against the advance of science, can be safely passed. Such a reply springs from the fatal serialism of the modern imagination—the image of infinite unilinear progression which so haunts our minds. Because we have to use numbers so much we tend to think of every process as if it must be like the numeral series, where every step, to all eternity, is the same kind of step as the one before. I implore you to remember the Irishman and his two stoves [he bought the first one because it would spend half the energy heating his house, so he bought the second one to halve the heating bill again and was surprised the heating bill was full price]. There are progressions in which the last step is sui generis — incommensurable with the others — and in which to go the whole way is to undo all the labour of your previous journey. To reduce the Tao to a mere natural product is a step of that kind. Up to that point, the kind of explanation which explains things away may give us something, though at a heavy cost. but you cannot go on 'explaining away' for ever: you will find that you have explained explanation itself away. you cannot go on 'seeing through things for ever. The whole point of seeing through something is to see something through it. it is good that the window should be transparent, because the street or garden beyond it is opaque. How if you saw through the garden too? It is no use trying to 'see through' first principles. If you see through everything, then everything is transparent. But a wholly transparent world is an invisible world. To 'see through' all things is the same as not to see.

The second mode — the song of experience that refuses to feed, thirst, clothe, heal, shelter, and visit (or ransom) because once upon a time someone took advantage of you, someone took your innocence — will not suffice either. It is this person, constantly looking out for themselves, who precisely misses Jesus. So too with the person convinced true malice does not exist: that the world isn't as thirsty, hungry, sick, exposed, shamefully naked, and convicted as it really is.

What did Jesus do? Was he naïve? Was he a tyrant simply trying to increase his "experience" of the "dark" side of the world? Did he submit to demonic hierarchies or try to build one for himself?

Nope.

He (1) says he is going to be murdered and (2) says it's not quite his time. He is nearly captured, stoned, stomped, stabbed, imprisoned, crucified, or flogged multiple times. Others try to get more food out of him. Still others ask him for money or healing or water.

Over and over again the text says he fed everyone, healed every disease, cast out every demon. Only a couple of times does he refuse these in order to point to a deeper desire, but even then it's because of a deeper gift he had on offer: his very death and very resurrection. He only refuses lower graces to the undeserving when he has higher graces to give. He only refuses to give you a fish when he's preparing a feast, not to give a snake.

Meaning, of course, that he wasn't naive and got blindly taken advantage of, but also wasn't jaded so that he "saw through" everything. He wasn't blind the other way. He didn't give to *no one* or have an excuse for not giving the majority of the time or refused to pray for miraculous healing or, worse, expected some favor or financial reward or pleasure or honor in return for what he gave. He literally commands us to give and expect *nothing* in return *to even our enemies*.

Eyes wide open, seeing a man *and what was in a man*, he did not entrust himself to men and also gave freely to them.

Eyes wide open for the joy set before him, Jesus endured the cross, scorning its shame, and sat down at the right hand of the Father.

That's wild.

"Wisdom is the recovery of innocence on the far end of experience." — Hart

KINDS OF GRACE.

I prefer other definitions of grace, but one of the most common defines grace as *unmerited favor*. To have favor you yourself did not merit. Like "do me a favor" you didn't merit or, in many cases, ask for. On our side, we have received everything. I live on support and often folks say things like I shouldn't beg. As if every other wage receiver in society doesn't beg. As if a pharmacy soliciting regular patrons isn't begging. As if conning old ladies into high cost, high commission mutual funds isn't begging. As if persuading the United States government to prop up the entire oil industry, the entire jet plane and bomb industry, the entire prison industrial complex, the entire big box retailer and e-commerce industry isn't begging. As if Taco Bell isn't begging people to buy their... well I won't call it food, but perhaps artisanal diarrhetics.

What do you think commercials *are*?

Everyone — and I mean everyone — is a beggar at the doors of the mercy of God and also the basic dirt of my Father's world. There isn't a father alive who provides for his kids so much as shuffles the provision of God from his hands into the hands of another. There aren't job creators. Just job shufflers. Creative types — artists and artisans — create ideas from component parts of creation, but even then they're still *borrowing* matter, ideas, causal chains, purposes from God. We build companies using roads and fire departments and telecom services *all of us built*. We build using natural resources God gives us. We steal ancient ideas that did not originate in our own minds.

You deserve none of what you have. You came naked, you leave naked. Jesus condescends into your mess and gives *you* a chance, of all people.

Why wouldn't you give it to someone else? Why not offer unmerited favor to the prisoner who did not merit freedom? Why not offer unmerited food to the hungry who did not merit sustenance? Why not offer unmerited favor to the thirsty who did not merit drink? To the naked who did not merit clothes? To the sick who did not merit healing? To the homeless who did not merit room at your inn? There was, in fact, no room for Jesus. No home for Jesus. No water for Jesus on the cross. No food for Jesus in the desert. No freedom for Jesus in chains.

No cure for Jesus dead on the slab *for three days*.

He says, though, even if folks don't merit it, because his merit didn't deserve the punishment — because he offers his grace by which The Father wills that all shall be saved — that if you give to those who *don't deserve it* to whom his merit extends from out of his undeserved suffering, you end up giving to him. When you give to them, you give to him. And often they end up giving — just like you — *as him*.

"I fill up in my body what is lacking in Christ's sufferings," said Paul.

St. Francis had the stigmata after a life of serving those who least deserved his peace and love and boundless joy.

Whatever you've done...

Whatever you've done...

Whatever you've done unto those who least deserve it. Unto those who have the least of it.

There's another thing about grace and mercy. Mercy withholds something negative. Grace tends to offer from one's self a positive that completely replaces and negates the need for even withholding the negative. Valjean's candlestick eradicated the need for the mercy of a reduced sentence. It goes beyond that: Jesus says it's no credit to anyone who gives to those who can return the favor. That is, at some time or another, all of us. He says it's a credit to you to give to those who cannot repay.

Of the various hungry, thirsty, naked, sick, exiled, imprisoned folk who exist, none have less ability to repay you than those who do not deserve it. Of all the prisoners who could return the favor, the truly guilty with a life sentence cannot repay. That's why the candlestick moment in Les Mis so moves us. The priest has no reason to give yet more silver to the man who stole it.

And yet he does.

And Valjean returns the favor to prostitutes, orphans, war criminals, and the rest.

Some when they encounter this idea of the undeserving least of the least realize that they, within themselves, have no capacity to give this much. They have too little strength, fortitude, long suffering. It's too hard. But then they encounter verses like "Blessed is he who dies in the Lord from now on for *his dead's live on after him"* -and *"I fill up in my body what is lacking in Christ's sufferings"* -and *"you are saved by grace through faith, not of yourselves, but as the gift of God in order to do good works."*

You start to realize it doesn't come from you after all.

Because YOU were the undeserving least. You were a beggar at the doormat of God Almighty. YOU were counted the worst enemy of Christ and yet he died for you anyways. From that grace, everything you do from here on out is cake: you don't pull on your strength. You pull on the strength you're in the present state of having been giving and continuing to get.

That's what makes forgiveness supernatural.

And it's why, according to Lazzo, 95% of exorcisms simply require forgiveness and reconciliation. No crazy prayers or rituals needed.

Forgiveness is just that powerful.

ENEMY LOVE.

The gospel would be easier if it existed just for my buddies, but I'm not that kind of Christian. In fact, I don't think that idea equates with Christianity at all. I don't fit in with most Christians because I believe in enemy love in my heart of hearts. I really and truly believe it and that's why I'm a Christian. That's why I consistently try to reach the people who are some of the hardest to reach in the world. By numeric metrics, Tara and I produce little fruit. By forgiveness metrics, however, I couldn't be prouder of the folks we have had the privilege of serving. But also: I'm the worst kind of hypocrite and therefore practice enemy love less than many who disbelieve in it. I do not do what I want to do. What I feel convicted to do.

To do what God did for us.

A friend recently bragged about how he was actively cutting virtually everyone out of his life who wasn't a close friend or someone he was reaching out to outside the church. He's a pastor. Bragged about it. A Christian pastor. I know for him, he's thinking about boundaries and his "true" friends and likely comparing it to his *idea* of me where he thinks I want to be liked by everyone. I did at one point, but violent personal attacks manifested in public one star book reviews (or email threats riddled with f-words) can cure that desire just as quickly as your home church's refusal to put your face on their wall of ministers. Both of which I've experienced. The truth is deeper: I don't see Jesus cutting people out of his life. Just the opposite. I see him saying I will *drag* all men to the Father, some of them kicking and screaming I suppose until the day they finally yield and bow with every other knee and turn and see what they truly protested all these years. I see him in the text in John's Gospel — who said in this way, not the cross, Jesus showed the fullest extent of his love — he washes the feet not only of all the friends he knew would soon abandon him. He washed the feet of the man Judas whom he knew would sell him out to the man, to the state, to the religious powerful mob for about a month and a half of unemployment checks.

Jesus didn't cut him out. Rather he washed the feet of the least of these twelve disciples. Washed Judas's feet to show the full extent of his love.

I understand boundaries have to be instated sometimes, I'm certainly getting better at it, but boundaries imply a border and a border implies the place where lands meet. Boundaries *require* presence and consequences for two people to meet. Solitary confinement or self-exile seldom imply boundaries. Rather, they imply a refusal to set boundaries. If the boundary is that I avoid you or cast you out of my presence for all time, it's not really a boundary, is it? It's just cowardice. There's a difference between the difference of persons — such as the intimacy of the Trinity where they defer, in unity, to one another: *I will drag all men to the Father, the Spirit conceives Jesus, the Father sends his son* — and the idea of the sea. Revelation says the day will come where there is no more sea: peoples and people will no longer be divided by anything other than the white stone with the unique, true name of their personhood. You will be united to everyone, you might as well start reconciling now and separating the wheat from the chaff in your own soul. Even that person you hate right now? Their true self will emerge one day and the chaff of their person will burn away, says 1 Corinthians 3. If Jesus says love your enemy and the person you hate the most is yourself, get to work.

Jordan Peterson and almost every cultural voice like him, liberal and conservative, does not help here. They say "love your enemies" means learn from them, take their tips, beat them in the long run. Use their strategy to defeat them on social media. That's literally the opposite of what Jesus says and means: when he says love, he means *love*. He means forgiveness. And you can see it by the way Jesus treats his enemy: you. While you were Jesus' foe, he died for you. It's cowardice to avoid or merely learn from our opponents.

What's harder is the long, slow slog of reconciliation. That takes patience. And it doesn't necessarily mean you *won't* cut someone out of your life for a year or two and then revisit. I did with my father and we reconciled before he died: he became a good man. Not only because of me, but because of several. It's never permanent because 1 Corinthians 3 among other places teaches us that we will have to deal with the healing, purging, and reconciliation of our relationships *anyways* when Jesus returns. We're stuck with each other — all of each other — forever. You've never met a mere mortal. Never once. You have to figure it out eventually. You can't hide your bitterness and stinginess and withholding of honor and cynicism forever.

We might as well get busy on the hard work of forgiving our enemies now. Sooner begun is sooner done, as Kvothe's father said. And that's a kid that could use some reconciliation.

Along those lines, Tara's granny passed during COVID and I wrote a threnody for her that *The Author's Journal of Imaginative Literature* bought. There's a stanza that goes:

> Now she knows the Hence and Hither
> From Whom all has gone;
> Sparrows fall, lilies wither,
> Yonder known by Yon;
> All the Want behind her wants,
> Longing known above;
> Knows if love be want to wander
> wandering to Love.

Be want to wander to love, friend.

Keep wandering down the path of love and reconciliation.

Works of Mercy.

I have been often tempted because of my deep conviction on this subject to tattoo the spiritual and corporeal works of mercy on my body as something like a task list: I figure if I do at least one that day, it's a good day. Love is the panacea. Love cures all, wins all, something like how exercise benefits all our body's systems, but beyond that to cure our whole humanity. They're based on the many verses in the books of scripture the church has chosen age after age:

Corporeal works of mercy

- feed the hungry.
- give water to the thirsty.
- clothe the naked.
- shelter the homeless.
- visit the sick.
- visit the imprisoned and ransom the captive.
- bury the dead.

Spiritual works of mercy

- instruct the ignorant.
- counsel the doubtful.
- admonish the sinners.

- bear patiently those who wrong us.
- forgive offenses.
- comfort the afflicted.
- pray for the living and the dead. (2 Tim 1:6-18;

I may well write more on these in the future, but I wanted to restrict myself to the words of Jesus in the specific passage because of his formulation. Maybe write those down and put them on your fridge. Put them on your heart. Impress them on your people and kin and neighbors and foes. Write them on the door frames of your house and on your gates. Talk about them when you sit at home and when you walk along the road, when you lie down and when you get up.

Heck, get a tattoo with some checkboxes by them and tick them off one or two with a bright green sharpie every day from out of the grace you've been given, from out of the life that brought you forth from your own grave.

All my unconditional respect, unconditional love, unconditional confidence from here until *The End*.

Lancelot of Little Egypt
Sunset Park
Brooklyn, NY
2021
soli Deo gloria
nunc dimittis

BIO.

Lancelot Schaubert has authored 14 books, 15 scripts, 40+ stories, 30+ songs, 60+ articles, 200+ poems, and a thesis for markets such as MacMillan (TOR), The New Haven Review (Yale's Institute Library), The Anglican Theological Review, McSweeney's, Writer's Digest, The World Series Edition of Poker Pro, Standard Publishing, and the Poet's Market — most recently his debut novel Bell Hammers, which he also narrated in theatrical audiobook.

He has ghostwritten and edited for NYT Bestsellers like Tim Keller, Brian Jennings, wrote the book proposal that sold Dr. Mark Moore's thesis (University of Prague) to TNT Clark, was the first to review Dr. Jordan Wood's The Whole Mystery of Christ: Creation as Incarnation in Maximus Confessor, wrote copy for large international nonprofit orgs and companies, and has served as an editor for bestselling fantasy authors Juliet Marrilier, Kaaron Warren, and Howard Andrew Jones for the anthology Of Gods and Globes (not to mention work as an senior editor for The Showbear Family Circus and a consultant for The Joplin Toad).

As a producer and director-writer, he co-reinvented the photonovel through Cold Brewed with Mark

Neuenschwander. That work caught the attention of the Missouri Tourism Board (as well as the Chicago Museum of Photography), who commissioned them to create a second photonovel, The Joplin Undercurrent; he also worked on films with Flying Treasure, WRKR, etc.; helped judge the Brooklyn Film Festival and NYC Film Festival; and he wrote, produced, and performed the symphonic novella All Who Wander. Spark + Echo selected him as their 2019 artist in residence, commissioning him to craft 8 fiction pieces that illuminated Biblical pericopes.

He's currently on assignment in Alaska for a documentary film, on assignment in Brooklyn for a potential criminal justice piece of journalism, and many other projects.

He lives and serves to help others make what they feel called to make: to that end he has raised over $400,000 in the last seven years for film, literary, audio, and visual arts projects as an artist chaplain in Brooklyn, New York. As he types this sentence, that means clipping the beard hairs of a dying theater producer and dealing with the estate administration for said producer's foster kids.

www.ingramcontent.com/pod-product-compliance
Lightning Source LLC
Chambersburg PA
CBHW030326100526
44592CB00010B/584